THE APPRAISAL OF

Readers of this text may be interested in the following related texts: *The Appraisal of Real Estate*, tenth edition; *The Dictionary of Real Estate Appraisal*, third edition; *Hotels and Motels: A Guide to Market Analysis, Investment Analysis, and Valuations*; and *Shopping Center Appraisal and Analysis.*

For a catalog of Appraisal Institute publications, contact the PR/Marketing Department of the Appraisal Institute, 875 N. Michigan Ave., Chicago, IL 60611-1980

**APPRAISAL
INSTITUTE**

THE APPRAISAL OF OUTDOOR *Advertising* SIGNS

Donald T. Sutte, MAI

Appraisal Institute
875 N. Michigan Avenue
Chicago, Illinois 60611-1980

Acknowledgments

Reviewers: Gene Dilmore, MAI, SRA

                Wayne Hagood, MAI

                Janice F. Young, MAI, RM

Vice President, Publications: Christopher Bettin

Manager, Book Development: Michael R. Milgrim, PhD

Editor: Stephanie Shea-Joyce

Manager, Design & Production: Julie Beich

For Educational Purposes Only

The opinions and statements set forth herein reflect the viewpoint of the Appraisal Institute at the time of publication but do not necessarily reflect the viewpoint of each individual member. While a great deal of care has been taken to provide accurate and current information, neither the Appraisal Institute nor its editors and staff assume responsibility for the accuracy of the data contained herein. Further, the general principles and conclusions presented in this text are subject to local, state and federal laws and regulations, court cases and any revisions of the same. This publication is sold for educational purposes with the understanding that the publisher is not engaged in rendering legal, accounting or any other professional service.

Nondiscrimination Policy

The Appraisal Institute advocates equal opportunity and nondiscrimination in the appraisal profession and conducts its activities without regard to race, color, sex, religion, national origin, or handicap status.

Library of Congress Cataloging-in-Publication Data

Sutte, Donald T.

    The appraisal of outdoor advertising signs / Donald T. Sutte.

      p. cm.

    Includes bibliographical references.

    ISBN: 0-922154-13-9

    1. Signs and signboards—United States—Evaluation.

2. Advertising, Outdoor—United States—Evaluation.. 3. Real property—Valuation—United States.   I. Title.

HF5843.S87 1994   93-36372

333.33'87—dc20   CIP

CONTENTS

	Foreword	vii
	About the Author	viii
	Introduction	1
Chapter One	The Signboard Industry	3
Chapter Two	Interests, Issues, and Court Ruling	8
Chapter Three	Appraisal Problems	16
Chapter Four	Types of Outdoor Advertising Signs	25
Chapter Five	Sign Characteristics for Valuation Purposes	30
Chapter Six	The Valuation Process and the Appraisal Report	39
Chapter Seven	Rating a Showing	52
Appendices	Traffic Audit Bureau Information	57
Appendix A.	Outdoor Visibility Rating System and Plant Operator Statements	59
Appendix B.	Standard Procedure for Evaluating the Circulation of Outdoor Advertising	68
Appendix C.	Vehicle Load Factor and Daily Effective Circulation	72
	Glossary	81
	Bibliography	92

FOREWORD

The valuation of outdoor advertising is an appraisal specialty that places great demands on real estate appraisers. To complete such an assignment competently, an appraiser must be knowledgeable about the locational and physical components of these unique properties and sensitive to the legal and political issues that engulf them. The appraiser must also be attuned to quantitative data, evaluating the ratings assigned to sign space within the industry, analyzing the supply of and demand for signboards, forecasting the cash flows accruing to sign owners, and allocating value among the individual signs in a group showing.

Written by an acknowledged expert in the appraisal of outdoor advertising, this text provides all the information an appraiser needs to know about these controversial properties. The structure and operations of the signboard industry are explored and the types and characteristics of both standardized and nonstandardized signs are described. Legal issues relating to property rights and just compensation are discussed in depth.

For appraisers seeking a general overview as well as those interested in the significant particulars encountered in the appraisal of outdoor advertising, this important text will prove essential.

Douglas C. Brown, MAI
1994 President
Appraisal Institute

ABOUT THE AUTHOR

$\mathcal{D}$onald T. Sutte, MAI, CRE, is the president and founder of Real Property Analysts, Inc. in Fort Lauderdale, Florida. Sutte holds a bachelor's degree in business administration from Florida Southern College and has 30 years of experience in the real estate field. He has written articles for the National Academy of Sciences, the Appraisal Institute, and the National Institute of Real Estate Brokers. As a licensed real estate broker and a certified general real estate appraiser, Sutte has provided consultation, appraisals, and expert witness testimony on a variety of subjects in all parts of the United States.

INTRODUCTION

*T*o estimate the value of signboards, a real estate appraiser must be familiar with the signboard industry as well as the physical and economic attributes of various signboard structures. An understanding of signboard rental, the types of advertisers involved, the factors motivating market activity, and the components of sales transactions is also essential. This text will explore these issues, define the property interests to be appraised, and document the principal methods of signboard valuation.

A variety of clients may require appraisal services. Most valuations of outdoor signboard structures result from governmental actions in eminent domain proceedings and, more recently, the imposition of amortization schedules. The amortization schedules imposed by some government agencies allow owners, usually sign companies, to keep signboards at their existing locations for the duration of the amortization period. Once the amortization period is over, however, the signs must be removed. The question of whether or not amortization reflects just compensation is a very difficult legal and appraisal problem.

The need to estimate just compensation stems from the removal of signboards necessitated by the Highway Beautification Act of 1965. The Highway Beautification Act has had an especially significant impact on the outdoor advertising industry because one of its goals was to enhance the scenic beauty of the American landscape through the elimination of signboards. The aesthetic merits of signboards and the usefulness of outdoor advertising are not the appraiser's concern. The appraiser's task is to analyze the actions of buyers and sellers in the marketplace and estimate the value of the legal interests being appraised. Research has revealed that distinct units of comparison are applicable to the valuation of signboards interests.

Readers should note that the appraiser's opinion of value is based upon whether the use of the property is legally conforming. Granted, many signs are either legally conforming or grandfathered, and thus exempt from the effects of current regulation. However, most standardized signs are legally conforming entities and this text is based on that premise. An appraiser of signboards must consider the marketplace, the actions of buyers and sellers, the many legal and appraisal ramifications of eminent domain proceedings, and, most importantly, the appraisal definitions of *market value* and *just compensation*.

The purpose of this text is to review all the factors affecting the valuation of outdoor advertising signs since the author's original text on this subject, *The Appraisal of Roadside Advertising*, was published in 1972. The earlier book considered the effects of the Highway Beautification Act of 1965 and specified a methodology for estimating compensation for the removal of outdoor advertising structures. Investigation of valuation concepts and the signboard industry over the years has supported the units of comparison recommended in the original text. Many of the problems that existed then continue to affect the market today. Like the 1972 study, this text presents acceptable, fair, and equitable valuation methods that can be used to estimate the market value of signboards.

Chapter One

THE SIGNBOARD INDUSTRY

The signboard industry is an advertising medium that relays messages to the general public like radio, television, or print media. Signboards are of two types: standardized outdoor advertising and nonstandardized, or on-premise, signs. The distinction between these two types of signs is important.

STANDARDIZED SIGNS

The standardized segment of the industry is represented by the Outdoor Advertising Association of America (OAAA) and the American Council of Highway Advertisers (ACHA). The Outdoor Advertising Association of America, located in Washington, D.C., is a trade organization of individuals and companies in the United States and abroad. The American Council of Highway Advertisers in North Beach, Maryland, is a similar organization of highway advertisers.

Both organizations represent the outdoor advertising industry in Washington, sponsor lobbying efforts on behalf of outdoor advertising interests, and conduct national and regional conferences.

Because the sign industry encounters much opposition in Washington and at state and local levels, lobbying is a major function of both organizations. Most trade and professional organizations have lobbyists who represent their interests. A case in point is the Appraisal Institute, which lobbied in Washington for appraisal reform, culminating in passage of the Financial Institutions Reform, Recovery and Enforcement Act.

Another important function of outdoor advertising organizations is to ensure the standardization of signs in terms of size and design. For example, poster panel signs throughout the country conform to certain standards of size and design. Uniformity of size and design allows a national advertiser to lease space on a signboard in much the same way as commercial time is purchased on television or radio.

In the standardized industry, many advertisers purchase (lease) space on a national basis. The same displays and copy may be seen simultaneously on signboards located in various parts of the United States. Standardized signs are generally located in urban areas or along interstate highways and well-traveled roads. Most are owned by sign companies which use their logo or name on the sign. Local businesses may also lease standardized signs to display their advertising or to relay directional information. Standardized signs include poster, junior poster, painted bulletin, and rotary paint signboards.[1]

NONSTANDARDIZED SIGNS

Nonstandardized signs generally are small, irregular in shape, and come in a wide variety of designs. They are often located in rural areas and are rarely leased by national advertisers. Many nonstandardized signs are directional or on-premise signs. As the name implies, a directional sign gives directions to a specific business. A certain percentage of directional signs are part of the standardized industry. As mentioned earlier, some local advertisers use standardized signs for directional information and local advertising campaigns.

Many nonstandardized signs are owned by individual shop owners or advertisers. The loss of such a sign can impact a business's operations. Compensation for the loss of this form of signboard is not considered in this text. On-premise signs are often located on service station, motel, and restaurant sites. They usually feature the name of the business and sometimes describe the services. On-premise signs are generally the property of the owners or occupants of the site.

Although it may sometimes be difficult to distinguish between standardized and nonstandardized signs, this distinction is very important from a valuation standpoint. One of the first tasks of the appraiser is to ascertain whether the sign is standardized or

---

1. For descriptions of these industry terms, the reader should consult the glossary.

nonstandardized. This question can usually be resolved very quickly by contacting the sign company identified on the face of the sign. The following pages show examples of both standardized and nonstandardized signs.

ON-PREMISE, NONSTANDARDIZED SIGN

ON-PREMISE, NONSTANDARDIZED SIGN

ON-PREMISE, NONSTANDARDIZED SIGN

STANDARDIZED AND NONSTANDARDIZED SIGNS

The signs in the center of the photo are poster panels and are part of the
standardized sign industry. The signs have the company name *Lamar*.
The sign advertising the furniture store in the background to the left is part
of a nonstandardized, on-premise sign group.

STANDARDIZED AND NONSTANDARDIZED SIGNS
The sign on the left in the background is a painted bulletin and is part of the standardized sign industry. The *Exxon* sign on the right is an on-premise sign.

Analyzing the type of sign and its location, ownership, and advertisement is very important in establishing the rent potential of the space. The quality and durability of the income stream form the basis for the sign's income-producing capabilities. In studying the income-producing characteristics of a sign, the appraiser also notes any differential that may exist between the rent (economic) the sign is capable of producing and the contract rental the sign is generating at the time of the appraisal.

Chapter Two

INTERESTS, ISSUES, AND COURT RULINGS

RECENT HISTORY

To understand the methodology applied in valuing outdoor advertising, appraisers should be aware of the recent history of the industry. Four different factors must be considered in signboard valuation.

1. Governmental initiatives or actions
2. Sign industry concerns
3. Courts and the law
4. Appraisers and appraisal methodology

Governmental Initiatives or Actions

Since passage of the 1965 Highway Beautification Act, government has been taking signs through various methods of acquisition. Both the general public and governmental agencies are aware that there are far fewer signs today than there were 20 years ago. With the prodding of the public and special interest groups, government has actively sought to remove all types of signs and discontinue the use of many locations for signboards.

Sign Industry Concerns

With government agencies attempting to remove signs, the sign industry perceives a threat to its survival and has shown some resistance. In response to increasing eminent domain litigation and the imposition of amortization schedules, the sign industry has focused on the issue of compensation. The concerns of the sign industry center around survival and just compensation.

Appraisers need not take sides on this issue. Their attention should focus on selecting appropriate appraisal techniques and interpreting the market to arrive at equitable compensation estimates.

Courts and the Law

The laws pertaining to the taking of signs and the rights of owners and users of signs are unclear. State and federal laws do not agree on what is being appraised and which procedures to apply in the valuation. In state courts the taking of signs may call for no compensation, full compensation, or something in between the two. The law is inconclusive. The practical aspects of estimating market value and the interpretation of outdated laws create a chaotic situation. Decisions are inconsistent but a variety of views are being heard in the courts.

Appraisers and Appraisal Methodology

In any valuation assignment, the appraiser must interpret market conditions and select appropriate valuation methodologies. By reviewing market trends, the appraiser can gain insight into the signboard market. In court proceedings, the legal issue of just compensation is paramount. To help in the estimation of compensation, appraisers are called upon to estimate value and provide testimony in court. Their valuation theories have often been challenged over the issue of whether signs are real property or personal property. While the judge may keep an open mind, it is the appraiser's task to interpret the market. With government regulations, the concerns of the signboard companies, and the courts to consider, the appraiser's task can become very difficult.

To interpret the market the appraiser must explore how signs are bought and sold in the outdoor advertising industry. An appraiser might interpret "the sale of signs" to refer to comparable sales data. In the sign industry, however, "the sale of signs" refers to the renting of sign space to an advertiser. To make use of this sale (rental) data, it is necessary to understand practical valuation techniques that all appraisers can apply. (It is assumed that the reader is an appraiser. Therefore, no attempt is made to teach basic appraisal methodology.) Before presenting the recommended methodology, some of the problems that arise in the appraisal of outdoor advertising signs will be reviewed.

PROBLEM AREAS

Four problems confront the appraiser:

1. State laws are not clear on whether signboards are personal property or real property.
2. The signboard industry is secretive and has been reluctant to provide appraisers with income data and sales information.
3. Many state and federal agencies do not fully understand the signboard industry and have not adopted modern appraisal concepts.
4. The signboard industry has been reluctant to litigate for their interests in the courts to establish a policy.

Personal Property or Real Property

Legal opinions pertaining to signboards conflict as to whether signboards represent personal or real property. To confuse the matter further, signs have sometimes been considered trade fixtures or chattels. This confusion has arisen from the need to estimate compensation. Federal law allows compensation for the expense of relocation and for complete removal of a sign. Therefore, the identification of signs as real or personal property has a great impact on the amount of compensation. If the signs are classified as personal property, compensation is restricted to a relocation expense.

The first test of the compensation issue is whether the sign can be relocated on the same site. To relocate a sign on the same site, four criteria must be met:

1. The new location is under the same ownership.
2. It is legally permissible to move the sign.
3. It is physically possible to move the sign.
4. The sign will have the same exposure (visibility) to traffic as before the relocation.

In most cases it is extremely unlikely that an outdoor advertising structure can be relocated on the same site with the same degree of utility. From an appraisal viewpoint, outdoor advertising signs must be considered real property because sign structures are affixed to the land and the right to use a signboard may be transferred through the creation of a leasehold interest.

Affixed to the land

Very simply, a sign structure is physically affixed to the land and has every indication of being a permanent structure. Construction details for a standard sign (its height and wind resistance) demonstrate that signboards are permanent structures affixed to the site.

Transferred through a leasehold interest

The term *leasehold* refers to the rights of the tenant who has leased the property from the owner. The leases pertaining to the land on which outdoor advertising structures stand reveal various long-term arrangements, from noncancellation leases to verbal leases that date back many years. A variety of cancellation clauses are included in land leases. (Cancellation clauses will be addressed in detail in Chapter 3.) The lessee's interest is part of the bundle of rights. The creation of leasehold interests to transfer signboards lends support to the contention that sign structures are real property. A sign on leased land is not unlike a building located on land held under a long-term lease.

Based on the attachment of sign structures to the site and the transferability of the use of signboards through the creation of leasehold interests, one can conclude that signs represent a real property interest.

Secretiveness of the Signboard Industry

In the past the outdoor advertising industry was very secretive about its sales transactions. Recently outdoor advertising companies have been more willing to share their sales data. These sales data are comparable to the sales data used in the appraisal of standard real estate and are essential to apply the sales comparison approach. Over the years the author has been able to obtain sales contracts and to interview buyers and sellers of outdoor advertising signs. Verification and use of sales information are necessary to derive sound value estimates in all appraisals. Reviewing both large and small sales of outdoor signs can provide insight into all aspects of the sales process.

Government's Understanding of the Signboard Industry

Since 1972 government has made considerable strides in learning about the signboard industry. State and federal agencies have developed a greater understanding of the outdoor advertising industry and how signs are bought and sold. Recent court settlements indicate that state and federal agencies have become more flexible in their attitudes regarding compensation. Courts and condemning agencies are now more aware of the motivations of buyers and sellers in the signboard market. When appraisers analyze signboard valuation issues, they consider the definition of market value used by the appraisal profession; the courts have not yet adopted a standard definition of market value to be used in the valuation of signs.

Litigation

Although the signboard industry was reluctant to litigate in the past, that attitude appears to have changed and there is now much litigation. Some of the current cases are very intense in nature. They have been initiated by outdoor advertising interests or forced on the industry by condemning action. By and large, the signboard industry collectively and signboard owners individually feel that their rights are being jeopardized. In many recent trials participants have been successful in establishing compensation based on analysis of the market, rather than reaching a settlement with some nonmarket formula.

Three summaries of court rulings in effect follow. All these rulings subscribe to the appraisal definition of market value. There seems to be general acceptance of compensation based on the valuation methodology presented in this text.

It has been demonstrated that a sign or signs constitute real estate. This premise is based on the sign structure's attachment to its site and the practice of drawing up land leases to transfer the right to use signboards. Unfortunately the law is still vague in many areas and will probably remain so for some time. By participating in court cases appraisers are involved in making law, using their experience in and understanding of the sign industry to establish useful precedents.

City of Scottsdale v. *Eller Outdoor Advertising Company of Arizona* (1978)

The *Eller* case involved the valuation of signs located within the City of Scottsdale, Arizona. These signs were valued with a gross income multiplier, a method of valuation considered especially appropriate by appraisers. The main question was the issue of compensation. This was one of the first signboard trials in which the court recognized the application of a multiplier as an appropriate valuation method.

Beaver Dam Raceway Inc. v. Town of Beaver Dam (1981)

This Wisconsin case related to the loss of a sign advertising a small racetrack. The appraiser in this case testified that the loss of the sign had resulted in a change in the highest and best use of the land and significantly affected its value. This case was one of the first in which the loss of an on-premise sign resulted in a change in the highest and best use of the land.

Dare County v. R.O. Givens, Inc. (1989)

At a recent trial in Nags Head, North Carolina, the sign owner requested compensation for signs that had existed on their sites for more than 30 years under verbal land leases. A gross income multiplier was used to arrive at a value estimate based on the assumption that the signs were on these sites for a long time and would, in all probability, have remained were it not for the condemnation action.

These cases resulted in new thinking on appropriate valuation methodology. All three involved full court proceedings with extensive documentation of the evidence presented by both parties.

CURRENT ISSUES

Three issues have become central to the outdoor advertising industry:

1.   The use of amortization schedules
2.   The estimation of business or real estate value
3.   Possible violation of constitutional rights

Amortization Schedules

Amortization schedules are the most recent method of removing signs. Their use is currently being tested in the courts. In a general context, an amortization schedule is a schedule of the time it will take for a debt to be repaid or a value to be compensated. Cities or counties impose amortization schedules that allow a sign company to maintain its signboards until a certain date, after which the signboards are to be removed without compensation. The courts have not yet decided whether the application of an amortization schedule is a legal issue.

From an appraisal viewpoint, however, applying an amortization schedule to signs reflects neither market conditions nor just compensation. If the sign represents a legal use (whether conforming or nonconforming), was granted a permit to be constructed, and is affixed to the land, it is very difficult to understand why fair compensation should not be offered. If this current trend continues, any real estate interest (e.g., a home, a retail store) condemned by a government agency may become subject to an amortization schedule.

Business or Real Estate Value

Some appraisers may find it difficult to ascertain whether a signboard constitutes business value or real estate value. Based on the author's experience, the real estate and business interests are quite similar. If the sign is a physical structure located on a site under a land lease, the sign is real estate. Moreover, a review of various market sales indicates that the interests in signboards that are not related to the real estate are relatively minor.

The author's investigation of numerous sales transactions involving thousands of displays indicated that the business interests were not significant and generally corresponded with the real estate interests. In fact, in most ways signboard sales are quite similar to transactions involving standard real estate. Business interests are certainly a part of outdoor advertising, but such interests need not be treated any differently in an appraisal than the business interests in large apartment complexes or office buildings. In the analysis of sales data, the term *business interests* surfaces continually. As applied to outdoor advertising signs, this term is synonymous with the real estate interests.

In analyzing a standard real estate transaction (e.g., the sale of an apartment building), the appraiser eliminates items that are not real estate from the sales data. Dollar adjustments are made for such items in the sales comparison approach to derive an adjusted sale price that reflects the real estate interests.

Violation of Constitutional Rights

The First Amendment to the U.S. Constitution guarantees the right of free speech. One could speculate as to whether the taking of signboard interests violates this right. The courts will rule on this matter. The Fifth Amendment to the Constitution, which is more directly relevant to the appraisal of signboards, states that private property cannot be taken for public use without just compensation. The amendment is spelled out fairly well in the Highway Beautification Act of 1965. Under eminent domain and condemnation litigation, private property can be taken only upon payment of just compensation. This, of course, is the crux of the problem—just compensation for signage. The author holds that if a government agency condemns signs, just compensation based on market value is warranted and necessary.

CONCLUSION

There are and will continue to be gray areas in the valuation of outdoor advertising signs. Legal interpretations and court rulings will affect the valuation of signboards in the future.

In court rulings pertaining to the appraisal of outdoor advertising, certain questions are repeatedly posed. These questions are

- Are signs real estate or real property?
- Are signs trade fixtures and chattels?
- Are the sign interests' rights to be considered a leasehold?
- Are relocation schedules appropriate?
- What are the proper methods of valuation?

Many, if not all, of these concerns are raised in every appraisal of signboards. The interpretation of these questions is often left to the real estate appraiser, who must answer them to apply the appropriate methodology. The appraiser is not expected to ignore legal interpretations, but is strongly urged to consider carefully the rights of property owners and current market conditions. If a fair estimate of just compensation is to be reached, the concerns of signboard interests must be addressed.

Chapter Three

APPRAISAL PROBLEMS

he Highway Beautification Act of 1965, sometimes called the Lady Bird Act because of the impetus provided by Lady Bird Johnson, was passed to enhance the scenic beauty of both rural and urban America. To implement the act, federal and local governments have made efforts to eliminate signboards, recommending either relocation or the payment of compensation for any signs that have been condemned.

For the past two decades, the sign industry and condemning agencies have been involved in litigation over the implementation of the act and the determination of the fair value of outdoor advertising structures. The legality of the signage is rarely in doubt. Local, state, and federal governments have long allowed signs to exist. Now these entities are threatening the continued existence of signs through eminent domain action or the imposition of amortization schedules.

RELOCATION

If a sign that has been condemned can be relocated on the same site, the appraiser should consider what constitutes reasonable compensation for relocation. In this case, the appraiser must ensure that the new location on the site provides the same visibility to the flow of traffic as the original location. The relocation of a sign or signs to unknown destinations cannot be considered fair compensation. In some instances condemning agencies have considered a relocation estimate as a method of compensation for the taking of 250 to 300 signs, but have not specified where these signs would or could be relocated.

Although many sign sites appear similar, it is extremely difficult to select an exactly equivalent site for relocation. Because more signs are being taken through condemnation and more governmental restrictions have been imposed on signs, the demand for quality sign locations has increased.

Signs have the characteristics of real estate, not personal property or trade fixtures, and location is as important to a sign as it is to other types of real estate. Before any estimate of compensation can be made, the exact location of the sign must be known.

WHOLE PROPERTY DEFINITION

It is imperative that the appraiser describe the method of valuation and define what constitutes the whole property. The form of ownership and location of the sign enter into this definition. For example, a group of signs owned by a national firm operating in different markets or locations may represent a whole property. Alternatively, the whole property may consist of an individual sign owned by a single entity. For valuation purposes, the relationship of the individual sign to the whole property must be established.

What constitutes the whole property is often dictated by the number of signs that are being purchased or condemned. In different markets, signs can be purchased either separately or by the thousands. Therefore, it is critical to define the whole property by determining whether the sign is a simple poster panel or one that rents as part of a larger group. For the most part, the standardized sign industry is characterized by metro markets in which a sign is typically rented either on an individual basis or as part of a group.

To estimate the value of the part taken or any damages to the remainder, the appraiser must analyze the whole property. Consider the valuation of a sign company's interests within the City of San Diego. The San Diego metro market consists of both the city itself and surrounding areas. Investigation revealed that, for appraisal purposes, the company's signs located throughout the metro area constituted the whole property.

Although the whole property included thousands of signs spread over the San Diego metro market, only the signs located within the City of San Diego were to be taken. One test of what constitutes a whole property is whether the signs can be rented individually or as part of a showing, i.e., a group of signs spread over a wide metro area. For practical purposes, signs can be sold (leased) on a individual basis, but in this case the whole property included all the company's signs in the San Diego metro market.

The terms *part taken* and *whole property* are associated with eminent domain proceedings or condemnation actions. Identification of the whole property will necessarily include consideration of the value of the part taken and any damages to the remainder.

The method of valuation applied in a given assignment is not dictated by legal considerations. The nature of the appraisal problem will determine the approach selected.

BUSINESS INTERESTS OR REAL PROPERTY?

In the valuation of outdoor advertising signs, business interests must be distinguished from real property. An investigation of numerous purchases of outdoor advertising signs across the country, in which the sign purchases constituted the total package, revealed that in the vast majority of the sales the purchase only included the signs themselves and appropriate land leases. In some situations, however, other items included in the sale must be considered. These items may include noncompete agreements; other forms of property on the site such as rolling stock, or vehicles; and possibly an office or plant building. The contents of a sale also reflect the advertising organization involved. A sale may consist of an individual sign without any trucks, paint plant, or personnel or, on rare occasions, it may involve a whole company which owns additional real estate interests. By and large, the sales data indicate that such additional items are not a significant consideration.

Signs are purchased for their locations, the signboard structures themselves, and the land leases that run with the sites on which the signs stand. These interests are quite similar to the real estate interests involved in the purchase of an apartment building, office building, or commercial center, which usually include the location, the physical structure(s), and the right to use the land under the lease agreement. Attributes such as advertising potential are related to locational interests. Location is of prime importance to all real estate assets, whether the real estate is residential, commercial, or industrial. This is equally true of the interests in outdoor advertising signboards.

Another element to be considered is political activism in the local area—i.e., the intensity of government involvement in sign regulation. In the appraisal process, this risk is reflected in the selection of a gross income multiplier and in the choice of comparable sales data. Land purchases are often subject to infrastructure exactions and legislative acts imposed by land use regulations or comprehensive plans. Thus, the sign owner faces problems similar to those encountered by land developers.

In short, the sale of interests in outdoor advertising signs and the sale of business interests are very comparable. It would be difficult to find any distinction between transactions involving real estate signs and those involving sign businesses. This fact can be demonstrated by analyzing sign sales transacted by large signboard companies or those that reflect large-scale purchases. If a sale includes unusual items, an appraiser can estimate their contributory value and deduct this amount in adjusting the sale price in the sales comparison approach. However, sign industry sales indicate that signs are real estate and do not reflect significant business interests. Comparing a sign property with another type of income-producing property will highlight the similarities and differences.

In the table below, the property interests and real estate characteristics of a standard office building and a rental sign structure are compared.

	Office Building (Rental)	Sign (Rental)
Type of ownership	Fee simple/ exception	Leasehold/ exception
Leasing of space	Yes	Yes
Leases or advertising contracts	Yes	Yes
Requisite maintenance staff	Yes	Yes
Leasing commission	Yes	Yes
Structure affixed to land	Yes	Yes
Management staff	Yes	Yes
Sales and promotional expenses	Yes	Yes
Legal and accounting fees	Yes	Yes
Depreciation schedule for tax purposes	Yes	Yes

The two property types are similar in all but the first category—i.e., the type of ownership. The title to an office building is generally held in fee simple and the land is owned by the building owner. There are notable exceptions; large office buildings have been constructed on leased land. In contrast, a sign structure is generally built on leased land, although here too there are exceptions and the land may be owned by the sign owner.

Office buildings lease space and signboards rent advertising space. An office building is rented with formal leases, while the sign interest uses advertising contracts. Office leases are generally of longer duration than advertising contracts. Both office buildings and signboards require maintenance staffs to keep the property (i.e., building or sign structure) in repair.

The office building management pays leasing commissions to affiliated brokers; the sign company pay an advertising agency for securing an advertiser. Both property types are affixed to the land, both have management staffs, and both incur sales and promotional expenses. Both property types have legal and accounting fees and both make use of depreciation schedules for tax purposes, but their methods of scheduling depreciation differ.

For tax purposes sign companies have been classified as businesses, but their business is real estate by its very nature.

THE SIGN MARKET

The market for outdoor advertising consists of buyers and sellers of signs. In the outdoor advertising industry, the term *buyer* refers to the person who rents the sign, in other words, the advertiser. Nevertheless, appraisers consider the actual sale (not rental) of signs and the interests in signs. Generally the buyers of signs seek the same interests as the purchasers of standard real estate. In the past some buyers used signboards as collateral to obtain leverage for financing. Other buyers hope to fill in a market—i.e., to expand into an area where they can sell or rent signboard space to national or local advertisers. Knowledgeable individuals may purchase sign companies and plants to enhance their own business interests. A small segment of the market is composed of purchasers of individual signs in specific locations. Especially well-located signboards may be bought on an individual basis and used as directional signs for real estate developments, restaurants, or lodging facilities.

The standardized sign industry is highly technical. The people who rent the space and sell the advertising copy must be specialists. The purchasers of individual signs and outdoor plants must also be familiar with local advertising needs. A portion of advertising originates with nationally known agencies, but advertising in individual markets is often directed by local agencies. A large percentage of people who rent signs in a particular metro market are from that area.

Signboards may be part of national advertising campaigns for car manufacturers and tobacco companies in which the same copy is used in locations across the country. In the industry, leasing by a national agency is known as a *national-type purchase* or *buy*. Purchases by national advertisers constitute a significant portion of local signboard leasing. Appraisers must be familiar with both national and local markets to determine which agencies are selling the advertising copy and leasing the signboard space.

Purchasers of outdoor advertising space are generally associated with the advertising industry. Comparable sales must be analyzed on a national, rather than a local, basis. One problem frequently encountered in litigation and trial proceedings is a lack of comparable sales within the same locality or state. Although local sales of outdoor advertising signs or plants may not be extensive, there are generally enough to provide acceptable comparables for appraisal purposes.

Formal Land Leases

In response to increased government restrictions, the sign industry has become more selective in the sites it uses and, over the past few years, more formal land leases have been employed. Written leases have generally replaced verbal leases. New sites for signboards are not easy to acquire because most cities, states, and counties have sign ordinances. Along federal highway systems, for example, there are legally prescribed intervals at which signs can be located. This is quite a departure from the days when signage could be constructed almost anywhere.

It is now recognized that the better the location, the greater the need for a strong land lease. Recently, the sign industry has begun to obtain long-term leases. However, in some areas (e.g., North Carolina) outdoor advertising interests based on verbal leases have been appraised. Signs may be located on sites for 30 to 40 years with no formal lease agreements. Obviously the strength of a lease depends on how long it has existed, the original intent of the parties, and how long the lease will remain in force.

Another factor to be considered is the likelihood that the site will be developed. The potential for development must be investigated so that the appraiser may assess the possibility that the land lease will be cancelled. Most sign leases have some type of termination clause. The appraiser must look beyond the letter of the lease to understand the intent of the parties and investigate how long the lease has been in existence. Valuation of the sign will depend on the risk associated with discontinuation of the lease. If a capitalization process is to be the valuation method, an income multiplier will be the appropriate unit of comparison and risk must be considered in selecting this multiplier.

Consider the land lease for a well-located site adjacent to a highly traveled interstate highway system. The sign is located on the site under a railroad lease. Railroads generally give licenses or leases to sign companies for sites in locations where signs will not interfere with railway operation. Railroad company leases usually have a 30-day cancellation clause. The site in question contains two outdoor advertising displays, which generate substantial rental income because of their highly visible location along an interstate highway.

At first glance this assignment would appear to be the valuation of a sign on land held under a lease with a short-term cancellation clause. In this case, however, there is an additional item to consider. The land under the railroad right-of-way is part of a large tract of railroad land that has potential for development as an industrial park. Therefore, the potential risk that the entire area will be developed must be considered. If the only place to locate the signs is on the land under the railroad right-of-way and no additional railroad land is available to relocate the signs, the choice of an income multiplier will be substantially affected.

Although most formal leases for signboards do have short-term cancellation clauses, the appraiser always must consider the highest and best use of the site—in the past, present, and future. In short, the appraiser considers both the length of time the sign has been on the site and the potential for future use of the site as a sign location.

Salvage Value

The salvage value of a sign is typically minimal in relation to its overall value. Parts of a sign may be used at another location, but the cost to take down a sign and reassemble it is generally prohibitive.

Unity Rule

In many cases the sign owner's interests have not been separated from the fee simple ownership of the property. Consider a convenience store that fully occupies its site. A lease agreement may exist between the convenience store owner and a sign company. In such a case, the sign usually takes up a small portion of the site and the rental income becomes part of the land/store owner's interest. Often the overall property value of the convenience store is estimated and the land lease itself is considered, but the actual sign is overlooked. By the very nature of the land lease, the sign has a right to be there, and the value of the sign should be identified as a separate and distinct interest.

This property includes a convenience store, a gas station, and a standardized sign.

Assume that the property value of the convenience store is $100,000. To value the sign interest, we must consider the income to the land/store owner from the land lease for the sign. The sign is located on the site by virtue of a land lease with a sign company. The site is completely occupied by the store and the sign. The improvements are of recent construction and it has been determined that the store and the sign represent the highest and best use of the property at present and for the foreseeable future. Using an appropriate valuation method, the value of the sign company's leasehold interest is estimated at

$30,000. Adding the $30,000 value of the leasehold interest to the $100,000 value of the property indicates a total value of $130,000.

If the store and sign represent the highest and best use of the property, both should have the same economic life. As a legally permissible use, the convenience store will continue to exist for the duration of its normal economic life. There is no reason to believe that the sign, which is also legally located, will not be allowed to continue its existence. Thus, the valuation must consider both the lessor's and the lessee's interest in the property, which may exceed what is normally considered in a fee simple interest valuation.

In this example, the land and convenience store are owned by one party, and the leasehold on the space and the sign represent the interest of the outdoor advertising company that owns the sign structure. If we assume that the highest and best use of this property is the convenience store plus the sign, it becomes apparent that we must value both the interest of the land/store owner and the interest of the sign company. If the appraiser does not consider the interests of the outdoor advertising company separately, the allocation of value between the land and the improvements will be incorrect since all property interests have not been considered. To test the validity of the conclusions derived, the appraiser should consider the length of time the sign has been located on the site and the intent of the parties to the land lease. The cancellation clause should not receive undue emphasis.

Chapter Four

TYPES OF OUTDOOR ADVERTISING SIGNS

ignboard companies that make up the standardized outdoor advertising industry rent (or, in industry usage, sell) advertising space to national and local advertisers. The outdoor advertising industry leases poster panels and painted bulletins of uniform shapes and sizes in markets throughout the country. The term *market* applies to the area in which the advertiser wants to promote goods or services. When signs are of uniform size and shape, advertisers can use the same advertising copy for displays in all areas of the country. In the nonstandardized sign industry, advertising copy is customized for individual signboards, particularly on-premise signs which may be of any size or shape. A nonstandardized sign is designed to obtain the best possible results for the owner-advertiser.

DISTINGUISHING CHARACTERISTICS

There are three primary types of signage—poster panels, rotary painted bulletins, and permanent painted bulletins. Variations within these categories include signs known as *junior posters,* or *mini-type posters.* Uniform sign sizes allow an advertising agency to purchase advertising space for the same copy in various locations and to target specific markets according to residents' income or life-style characteristics. The following tables describe the various forms of outdoor advertising.

Posters

Descriptions	Chief Characteristics	How Leased	Special Features	Other Comments
Standard panel size 12ft. x 25ft., lithographed or silk screened then prepasted and applied to the poster panel's face on location.	Placed along primary, secondary, and tertiary arteries to provide simultaneous coverage in different market segments.	Leased by group or showing: a number of panels through-out the market bought as a unit. Customarily leased on a 30-day basis.	Illuminated in high circulation locations.	Represent the greatest number of signs in the industry nationwide.

Painted Bulletins

Descriptions	Chief Characteristics	How Leased	Special Features	Other Comments
Large advertising structure, generally 14ft. x 48ft. Copy is painted directly on surface.	Placed in premium locations with relatively high circulation.	Advertising space usually sold on an individual basis. Can be permanent (copy stays in one location) or rotary (copy moves to different locations every 60 days.) Leased on a 4- to 36-month basis.	Illuminated. May have cut-outs or embellishments attached to the face to extend the sign beyond standard area or to provide a three-dimensional effect.	Generally the most effective in the top 100 markets. Located along primary arteries and at intersections of freeways. Usually repainted every 6 or 12 months.

Spectaculars
Painted Bulletins Embellished with Electrical Effects

Descriptions	Chief Characteristics	How Leased	Special Features	Other Comments
Special steel construction, built to order.	Placed in an area with heavy night auto traffic. Most costly form of sign. Each one specifically fabricated. Most conspicuous of all outdoor advertising.	Individually. Price of construction, rental, and maintenance individually negotiated.	Everything built to order.	The costliest form of outdoor advertising. Usually bought on a three- to five-year basis because of high cost of construction. Change of copy costly.

One common feature of poster panel and painted bulletin signs is of particular importance to appraisers. Both can be rented (sold) as part of a package or group of signs or they can be rented on an individual basis.

Poster panels can be sold individually, but most often they are sold in a group known as a *showing*. (See Chapter 7 for further discussion of showings.) A typical poster panel is 12 feet by 25 feet, illuminated, and placed at a high circulation location with excellent exposure to the market. Many people will view the advertising message within a 24-hour period. It should be noted, however, that the value of a sign is not measured strictly by the number of people who will view it. The advertising message must be placed at a location where it will be seen by individuals who are able to buy or use the product advertised. High traffic volume alone does not make a location good.

Another common form of outdoor advertising, the painted bulletin, is a larger sign, usually measuring 14 feet by 48 feet. These signs are generally illuminated, with or without special embellishments. The painted bulletin may be either a permanent paint or a rotary paint. While the copy on a permanent paint remains unchanged, the copy on a rotary paint circulates among different locations every two months. A rotary paint bulletin is designed in sections. The sections are painted and assembled on site and, after two months, they are taken down and transported to another location within the metro area.

In the valuation of a poster panel or a painted bulletin, the appraiser must be aware of how the specific sign being appraised is rented to ascertain whether it is generating appropriate income.

PHYSICAL STRUCTURE AND TERMS

The following exhibits show the construction components of a painted bulletin and a standard poster panel.

PAINTED BULLETINS

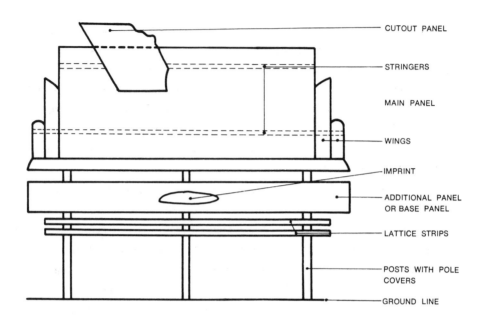

- CUTOUT PANEL
- STRINGERS
- MAIN PANEL
- WINGS
- IMPRINT
- ADDITIONAL PANEL OR BASE PANEL
- LATTICE STRIPS
- POSTS WITH POLE COVERS
- GROUND LINE

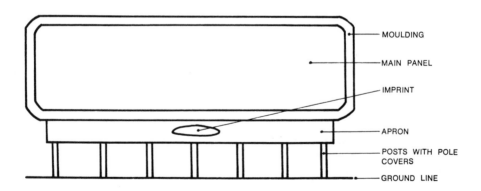

- MOULDING
- MAIN PANEL
- IMPRINT
- APRON
- POSTS WITH POLE COVERS
- GROUND LINE

STANDARD POSTER PANEL

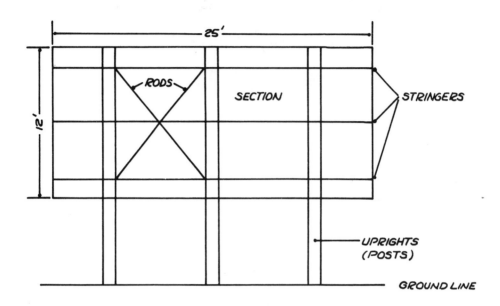

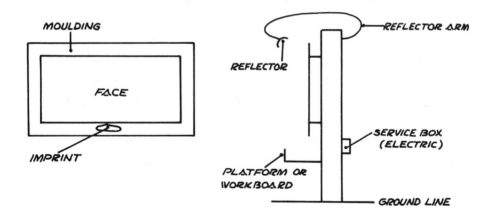

Chapter Five

SIGN CHARACTERISTICS FOR VALUATION PURPOSES

*T*he photographs on the following pages depict various types of signs and sign structures that the appraiser may encounter in performing valuation assignments. Also included are three photographs (on pages 37 and 38) showing the placement of sign identification numbers. Several of the photos are accompanied by suggested appraisal procedures, which indicate important points to be considered in the appraisal of this type of signboard.

The signs in the photographs are posters and painted bulletins. Apart from minor variations in size and shape, poster and painted bulletin signboards are fairly standard throughout the outdoor advertising industry. Signs sometimes described as junior posters may, in fact, be odd-shaped painted bulletins. Nevertheless, all standardized signs have similar characteristics and, from an appraisal perspective, may be valued by means of a common methodology.

STANDARD POSTER PANEL
This sign displays advertising copy for a fast-food restaurant.

Appraisal Procedures: This poster panel has most likely been leased as part of a showing. The advertising on the sign indicates who the lessee, or income generator, is. This sign may have been rented as part of a national or local advertising campaign.

STANDARD POSTER PANELS
These signs show directional copy that refers the viewer to the location of the advertiser.

Appraisal Procedures: These poster panels are part of a local buy—i.e., the space has been leased by a local advertiser. The copy relates to an advertiser located within the immediate area. These signs may or may not be rented as part of a showing or group of signs. The appraiser should investigate both contract rent and market rent.

STANDARD POSTER PANELS
The advertising messages on these signs reflect two different types of advertisers. The sign on the left is probably part of a national purchase to promote a motion picture. The sign on the right bears directional information provided by a local auto dealer.

Appraisal Procedures: The appraiser should investigate the source of income for the signs and their market rent. The sign on the left is most likely part of a showing, while the sign on the right is a single purchase. Although the two sign faces are located at the same place on the same street, they may be leased on very different bases. Therefore, it is important that the appraiser know to whom the signs are leased in the market.

STANDARD POSTER PANEL

The copy on this sign advertising Montclair cigarettes indicates that it is
a national purchase. The sign is part of a showing.

Appraisal Procedures: The income produced by this sign should be investigated. If the appraisal problem warrants, it may also be necessary to rate the showing. (See Chapter 7.)

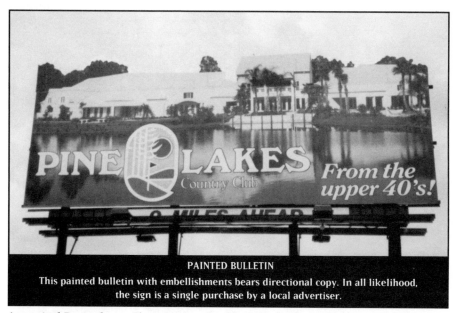

PAINTED BULLETIN

This painted bulletin with embellishments bears directional copy. In all likelihood,
the sign is a single purchase by a local advertiser.

Appraisal Procedures: The appraiser should establish the contract rent to the sign and estimate the market rent. This sign is a permanent painted bulletin and cannot be part of a showing.

PAINTED BULLETIN

This painted bulletin without embellishments may or may not have been sold as part of a rotary paint showing. (In a rotary paint showing, sign copy is circulated every two months.)

PAINTED BULLETIN

This is a standard painted bulletin with embellishments.

PAINTED BULLETIN
This painted bulletin with embellishments is part of a national purchase.

PAINTED BULLETIN
This painted bulletin is a local purchase.

PAINTED BULLETIN
This sign with embellishments is part of a national purchase.

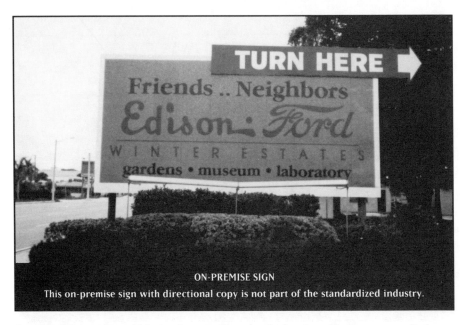

ON-PREMISE SIGN
This on-premise sign with directional copy is not part of the standardized industry.

Appraisal Procedure: This sign is owned by a local advertiser. The income-producing potential of the sign should be investigated.

These final photos show the placement of permit numbers and other information that can help an appraiser identify the owner of a sign.

State tag number AY 347
560 is the sign company's identification number

The company code number is shown in the lower left corner of the sign.

The company sign number is located in the lower right corner of the sign.

The appraiser should understand the characteristics of various signs. If the signs being appraised are part of the standardized sign industry, the appraiser should investigate the contract rent and estimate the appropriate market rent. It is also important to determine whether the panel is leased on an individual basis or as part of a showing. Painted bulletins should be identified as permanent paint or rotary paint. This information is available from signboard companies.

In addition to tracking sign income, sign companies publish a rate book containing information on the various types of signs and how they are leased. Rate books list the number of signs a company owns and the cost for different showings. Showings will be discussed in more detail in Chapter 7.

Chapter Six

THE VALUATION PROCESS AND THE APPRAISAL REPORT

efore a real estate appraiser attempts to estimate the value of a sign, he or she should review the definitions of basic appraisal terms such as *market value, leasehold, leasehold interest, the bundle of rights,* and *the principle of substitution.* The definition of market value establishes the basis for valuation. Simply stated, market value reflects what a willing buyer will pay and a willing seller will accept in payment for the real estate. Since we have concluded that sign interests represent real estate, the market value definition is extremely important to the final estimate of value.

Leasehold and leasehold interest refer to the right that is being conveyed. In nearly all signboard sales, the right to locate and use the sign structure is conveyed by lease. These property rights are associated with the leasehold interest. Market data indicate that most signs are located on land held under either short- or long-term leases. Therefore, the leasehold interest in a particular property or location is very important. The leasing arrangement is reflected in the price paid for the real estate. Included among the bundle of rights in real estate is the right to lease or to convey the leasehold interest. The bundle of rights concept provides that the right of use can be separated from the fee simple ownership.

The principle of substitution reflects the actions of buyers and sellers in the market-place and is applied in all three approaches to value. The principle of substitution states that when several similar or commensurate commodities, goods, or services are available, the one with the lowest price will attract the greatest demand and widest distribution. In estimating the value of outdoor advertising signs, the principle of substitution is embodied not only in the cost approach, but also in the sales comparison and income approaches to value.

PURPOSE AND USE OF THE APPRAISAL

In any estimation of value, the appraiser should understand the purpose and use of the appraisal. The appraiser must identify what rights are being taken and for what compensation is being estimated. To appraise a single sign, the appraiser has to know whether the sign is part of a larger parcel or parent holding. If it is part of a group, are all the signs being appraised as of a specific date? Will the taking of some of the signs damage the value of any remaining signs? Thus, in the initial stages of the assignment, the purpose, use, and date of the valuation must be established.

Most outdoor advertising signs are part of a larger parcel or parent holding. The value of a specific sign may be self-contained or it may derive from being part of a group of signs being rented. If the sign is part of a group, the appraiser must ascertain how these signs are leased. Is a separate lease signed for each sign or is the group covered by one lease? Without this information it is impossible to determine which interests are being taken or to arrive at a reasonable estimate of just compensation.

THE APPRAISAL PROCESS

In the appraisal of signboards, all three approaches to value should be considered. The cost, sales comparison, and income approaches vary in their applicability to any given problem. In most cases all three approaches cannot be effectively applied nor will they always reflect market thinking. Since the market provides the basis for the appraiser's opinion of value, it is essential that the approach to value applied be based on interpretation of the market. In the valuation of outdoor advertising, the sales comparison approach is the principal approach to be considered. Each of the approaches is described below and the components of the approach that may be applicable to sign appraisal are highlighted.

Cost Approach

The cost approach may be used to value nonstandardized signs and on-premise signs. An on-premise sign is generally located on the business site and the copy displayed refers to that business or location.

Although the cost approach is sometimes used in the appraisal of nonstandardized signs, it should be applied with extreme caution. Three shortcomings of the cost approach are explained below.

1. *Does not reflect market thinking.* The buyers and sellers of outdoor advertising do not consider the replacement cost of a sign, minus depreciation, as an accurate estimate of value when they purchase signs.
2. *Depreciation may be impossible to estimate.* Because sign companies are continually refurbishing sign structures, standard methods of estimating physical depreciation cannot be applied to outdoor signs. In addition, cost estimating services do not develop age-life tables for signboards as they do for other categories of real estate. Moreover, economic obsolescence attributable to negative external influences is extremely difficult, if not impossible, to estimate.
3. *Replacement cost may not reflect value.* The replacement cost of a sign can be estimated quite readily. The actual cost to build a sign can be determined from contractors' estimates or bids. However, the cost of acquiring the site for sign usage must also be reflected in the cost estimate. Companies continually acquire new sites for outdoor advertising. To complicate matters further, associated costs for items such as entrepreneurial profit must be estimated.

In summary, it may be very difficult to apply the cost approach. Estimates of physical depreciation and economic obsolescence may be impossible to derive. Most significantly, buyers and sellers in the market generally do not consider cost in the sale or purchase of signs.

Income Approach

Both standardized and nonstandardized signs are leased for rental income. Because the use of signboard space is conveyed as a leasehold interest, signs may be considered real estate and the income approach may be adapted to their valuation.

Appraisers should note, however, that one traditional application of the income approach, direct capitalization of net operating income, is not a justifiable method of valuation for signboards. A review of sales data and leasing transactions indicates that the capitalization of a net operating income estimate based on expense ratios is inappropriate. As time passes and more information on expense ratios is obtained, this method of valuation may become valid.

In many communities, appraisers and local property assessors keep data on expense ratios for different types of real estate. Real estate management agencies and associations may also serve as information sources, providing expense ratios, capitalization rates, and other data relevant to the local market. As of this writing, comparative data on the income and expenses of signboards are not available. The operating expenses and expense ratios obtained from large and small companies within the sign industry vary, so comparisons are difficult. Signboard sales also show great variance in expense ratios. No specific data are available to justify the selection of expense ratios. Industry sales also vary considerably and may reflect transactions involving only one sign or sales of thousands of signs. Thus, expense ratios, occupancy factors, and capitalization rates are difficult, if not impossible, to estimate.

In the income approach, the appraiser must arrive at estimates of both contract rent and market rent. Contract rent and market rent are not synonymous. Information on contract rent can be obtained from sign company records; market rent must be derived from current rate sheets or from a comparison of sign rentals.

The appraiser must also investigate occupancy factors, which may relate to a single sign or a group of signs. An occupancy factor is the ratio between the income derived from the rental units currently occupied and the income that would be derived if all units were occupied. Market rent and occupancy factors are fundamental to the income approach in the valuation of outdoor advertising signs. As more information becomes available, we may in the future be able to develop capitalization rates similar to those used in appraising other forms of real estate.

Sales Comparison Approach

The sales comparison approach is most applicable to the valuation of outdoor advertising signs. The information needed to apply the sales comparison approach is obtained from market transactions that represent the negotiations of buyers and sellers in the market. While all three approaches to value are based on market comparisons and market data, the sales comparison approach is the key to the valuation of outdoor advertising signs. Numerous transactions characterize the outdoor advertising market. Because this market encompasses many different locales, appraisers must review and compare sales data from all over the county. The relevant unit of comparison applied in the sales comparison approach is the gross income multiplier (*GIM*).

Gross income multiplier

In the sales comparison approach, sales data are analyzed to develop a gross income multiplier. This gross income multiplier is then used to capitalize income. Before developing a multiplier, the appraiser must estimate the potential market rent of the sign or signs and review their effective gross income. The rental income estimate may relate to either an individual sign or a group of signs, depending on the appraisal problem.

The appropriateness of using a gross income multiplier to appraise signboards is based on a number of observations, which are discussed below.

Use of the GIM in the sign industry

Participants in the outdoor advertising industry focus on the gross income multiplier. The multiplier is a rule of thumb used by buyers and sellers to arrive at the value of a sign for purchase or sale. Gross income multipliers are widely used in real estate appraisal because they 1) are applied by market participants, 2) are generally understood by real estate appraisers, and 3) reflect market conditions.

Expense ratios

An operating expense ratio cannot be derived from sales data. In the appraisal of apartment and office buildings, an abundance of operating information can be obtained from local assessors' offices and real estate publications. The appraiser also has access to a number of cost-estimating services which provide various costs based on units or ratios. By analyzing comparable expense ratios, appraisers can extract and compare capitalization rates for most properties. Such data are not available for signboards. After a review of signboard sales and income data, attempts to derive operating expense ratios from them have been inconclusive.

It is very difficult at this time to estimate what may be considered a standard operating ratio. The use of the multiplier takes into consideration a variety of expense ratios. Studies have indicated an acceptable range of market-derived multipliers. Therefore, valuation estimates can be derived through the use of multipliers.

Adaptability to a single sign or group of signs

Gross income multipliers can generally be applied to both single signs and groups of signs. In fact, gross income multipliers are useful in solving many appraisal problems encountered in the appraisal of outdoor advertising. By contrast, an appraiser who analyzes an individual sign and attempts to capitalize its net income will find it impossible to develop a market-derived capitalization rate.

Consideration of risk

When sales information is analyzed, a range of multipliers is usually found. Over the years this range has generally been found acceptable by appraisal standards. That is to say, the sales data indicate a range of multipliers that remains relatively constant. This text does not supply specific multiplier information because multipliers do change. Multipliers can be readily derived from current sales information. However, the multipliers applied to outdoor advertising are generally lower than the multipliers applied to standard real estate such as office buildings, apartments, and retail stores because signboards carry a greater degree of risk. This risk factor is inherent in renting the locations for signs. The lower multiplier reflects the greater risk associated with the investment.

Selecting the multiplier

Many factors must be considered by the appraiser in selecting an appropriate multiplier for a signboard. The areas to be investigated include:

1. Governmental attitudes
2. Site locations (highest and best use of the sites) and land use trends
3. Type of advertising copy displayed
4. Demographics of the area

Governmental attitudes

Governmental attitudes toward signboards, especially any hostility that may precipitate the removal of signs, have an impact on the gross income multiplier selected. Obviously, if a governmental body is being urged by environmental groups to ban outdoor advertising in a specific location, the risk associated with signs at that location will increase significantly. Thus, a lower multiplier would be selected to reflect the risk.

Site locations (highest and best use of the sites) and land use trends

Signs may be located in an area where the highest and best use of sites is changing and the signs may have to be removed for development. This possibility could influence the selection of the multiplier. The appraiser should determine how long the signs have been located on the site and estimate their remaining life. Such an estimate is based on land use trends in the area.

Types of advertising

The type of advertising copy displayed on the sign may also be of importance. The advertising copy may indicate a purchase by national buyers when the trend has been for local advertisers to lease signboard space. The appraiser should be aware of how such a trend could affect the signboard's value. The durability and quality of the income derived from leasing the signboard must be considered.

Demographics of the area

The demographics of the area also influence the risk associated with signboards, which affects the multiplier selected. In any property valuation, economic trends are an important market consideration, specifically trends relating to the purchasing power of the local community. If the outdoor advertising signs are located in an area where employment is declining, this can impact the multiplier. An overview of area demographics, including population growth or decline, household income, and the employment base, will be useful to the appraiser.

Experienced appraisers of outdoor advertising have discovered that the gross income multiplier is the appropriate unit of comparison to be applied in the sales comparison approach. It reflects the risk perceived in the market and is applicable to individual signs as well as groups of signs.

COMPARABLE SALES INFORMATION

Sales data provide the basis for any valuation estimate. The following list outlines the informational items to be considered in the appraiser's analysis.

1. *Location of the sales*

    Common address of site location along a street or highway; city, county, and state

2. *Physical data*

    Description of the type of sign or signs—e.g., painted bulletin, poster

3. *Grantor*

    The seller of the sign or sign interest—i.e., the leasehold interest

4. *Grantee*

   The purchaser of the individual sign or sign interest

5. *Sale price*

   The price paid for the signboard when it was sold

6. *Sale date*

   The date the sale was transacted

7. *Rolling stock*

   Items such as trucks and vehicles. It is important to know if any rolling stock was included with the transfer of the property.

8. *Other real estate*

   Occasionally additional real estate holdings that do not contribute to the rental of signs are included in a transaction. If such real estate is included, it should be separated from the sign interest and an adjustment made to the sale price. The sign company may own some individual sites with a highest and best use restricted to signs only. This land use characteristic should be noted.

9. *Land leases*

   It is important to verify the type of land lease—long-term or short-term—and to determine if any cancellation clause is included, for what period, and for what purpose. The appraiser should compare the provisions of the land lease with the terms customary in the community.

10. *Noncompete agreement*

    A noncompete agreement restricts the seller of the sign or signs from building or leasing sign space within a given area for a specific period of time. If a noncompete agreement is included in a transaction, the appraiser should determine if any monetary value was attached to this agreement.

11. *Goodwill*

    Goodwill is sometimes reflected in a sign sales transaction. A dollar amount may or may not be attributed to goodwill. This should be investigated. Goodwill is usually an item of bookkeeping or a tax consideration.

12. *Income figures*

    To select a gross income multiplier appropriate to the appraisal problem, information on the effective gross income of the outdoor advertising structure as of the sale date must be gathered. This information corresponds to the income data analyzed in the appraisal of apartment complexes, office buildings, and retail stores. A verifiable effective gross income estimate should be included with the sales information.

13. *Source*

The source of the data and corroborating verification

14. *General comments*

Any additional information required to explain the valuation problem and the appraiser's conclusions.

VERIFICATION AND INTERPRETATION OF SALES DATA

In analyzing sales data, it is extremely important to verify the terms and conditions of the sale. Equally important is the precise identification of what constitutes the real estate, in this instance, the leasehold plus the structures.

Two non-real estate items that may be specifically mentioned in the sales data are goodwill and noncompete agreements. In many transactions specific dollar amounts are allocated to these items. In verifying sales data, the appraiser should check deductions for goodwill and noncompete agreements since adjusted sale prices are used to arrive at the final value estimate. The verification of transactional data and the proper interpretation of comparable sales information ensure a supportable value estimate. Sales contracts should be reviewed and all data should be verified to the greatest extent possible.

A review of comparable sales of outdoor advertising signs reveals many similarities in the types of properties being sold. The vast majority of the conveyances include items that qualify as real estate only. Items such as copyrights and patents should be excluded from the sales data; only items of real estate should be included in the comparable sales analysis. Obviously the items included will vary from sale to sale, and the appraiser must make appropriate adjustments. The foundation of any appraisal is the comparable sales data and the verification process.

TRENDS WITHIN THE SIGN INDUSTRY

Whether the appraisal is of one sign or a plant consisting of many signs, the appraiser should consider industry trends that affect supply and demand within the market area. Specifically, these trends include the number of new builds and takedowns, company or plant income, and political considerations.

Number of New Builds and Takedowns

The phrase *new builds and takedowns* refers to the number of new signboards that are being constructed and those that are being removed, generally because of new real estate developments or highway acquisitions. Historical data on new builds and takedowns within the general market area are analyzed by the appraiser in selecting a multiplier. In past years the balance between new builds and takedowns has generally indicated that more signs are being taken down than are being built. The appraiser should investigate the direction of this trend in the specific market area.

Company Income or Plant Income

Historical data on the income a sign company receives indicate the profitability of the signboards. An increase or decrease in market rents affects the potential rental income of all signs and indicates the direction of rental trends.

Political Considerations

The appraiser should also consider how local government views outdoor advertising. Are amortization schedules being put into place? Is there increased interest in the removal of signs? Will signs be allowed to remain under some type of compromise arrangement? Political considerations such as these are important in the appraisal of signboards just as the government's attitude toward development is critical to the valuation of vacant land.

THE APPRAISAL REPORT

Appraisal reports should meet the requirements of the Standards of Professional Appraisal Practice of the Appraisal Institute. A report communicating the appraisal of outdoor advertising signs will often have special characteristics that reflect the particular assignment. The following items would be found in an appraisal report for an outdoor advertising sign. This list is not all-inclusive and the appraiser may find that some items need to be added or expanded.

1. Letter of transmittal
2. Description of the sign plant (if applicable)
3. Location and physical characteristics of the sign or plant
4. Date of valuation
5. Methodology to be applied
6. Rental history (rent stipulated in leasing contract)

7. Land lease brief
8. Occupancy factors
9. Comparable rentals (to establish market rent)
10. Comparable sales
11. Application of approaches to value
12. Plant income and occupancy factors (if applicable)
13. Reconciliation

The valuation process must be adapted to the specific problem and the methodology applied must be documented in the appraisal report. The Standards of Professional Appraisal Practice should be observed at all times.

The appraisal report provides support and documentation for the value estimate. The most important items in reporting the appraisal of signboards are the analysis and verification of sales information. The comparable sales should be adjusted so that their adjusted prices reflect only the leasehold interest and the sign structure itself. Proper consideration of market rent is also essential to derive an accurate value estimate.

The essential components of an appraisal report are discussed in the following section.

Letter of transmittal

The letter of transmittal sets forth the purpose and use of the report and the date of value.

Description of the sign plant

If the valuation problem so requires, the report may include a description of the sign plant and consider additional facts such as

- The metro market served
- The number of employees in the sign company
- Plant locations
- General descriptive or historical information on plant ownership (e.g., number of faces, types of faces, occupancy rates, trends, number of new sign permits, breakdown of sign locations)

This section of the report acquaints the reader with the plant and the relationship among the individual signs being valued.

Location and physical characteristics of the signs or plant

The location and physical characteristics of the signs should be briefly described in the appraisal report. Location can be identified with a common street address or the names of the streets where the sign is located. The date of construction, type of construction, and any other information pertaining to the physical characteristics of the structure should be provided as well.

Date of valuation

The date of valuation establishes the date for which the value estimate is valid.

Methodology to be applied

The report should describe the methodology to be applied early on to familiarize the reader with the interests involved and the methodology that the appraiser has selected to solve the problem.

Rental history

The rental history of each individual sign is described. If the sign is part of a group of signs, it may be necessary to explain how the sign has been rented.

Land lease brief

Generally, signs are located on leased land, so there should be a record of the length of time that the sign owner has held a lease with the landowner. It is essential that the report establish how long the sign has been located on the property and the likelihood that it will remain on the site. The terms and conditions of the lease should be discussed in the report.

Occupancy factors

Occupancy factors determine the amount or percentage of rental income that the individual sign has generated; they are basic to an understanding of the sign's income-producing potential.

Comparable rentals

The comparison of market rent to contract rent is very important in the valuation of any income-producing property. Comparable rentals must be analyzed to estimate a sign's rental income.

Comparable sales

Comparable sales are gathered in the market and analyzed in the appraisal. Such sales data must be verifiable.

Application of approaches to value

In most signboard appraisals, the sales comparison approach will be used. The sales analyzed are often national because local sales may be difficult to find.

Plant income and occupancy factors

The circumstances of the assignment will determine whether the report needs to include plant information. Plant information refers to:

- The income the plant has generated in the past
- The number of takedowns and new builds
- Factors affecting the economic viability of the plant
- Any trend that may influence the value of the sign

Reconciliation

The data, methods, and value indications derived in the appraisal must be reconciled in the report. In the reconciliation section of the appraisal report, the appraiser leads the reader logically through the analytic process applied to arrive at the final value conclusion.

Chapter Seven

RATING A SHOWING

THE APPRAISER'S INVESTIGATION

A poster panel is generally sold or rented as part of a group of signs, which is known as a showing. Investigation of the plant records kept by the sign company or owner will reveal how the sign being appraised has been rented (or sold in industry terminology). The rating of a showing is generally undertaken when an individual poster panel is being appraised. If the subject sign is typically rented as part of a showing, the showing must be rated to estimate the income attributable to the sign.

Answering the following questions can help the appraiser determine whether it is necessary to rate the showing:

- How was the individual sign rented (sold) in past years?
- Could the sign be rented for a greater amount if it were not part of a showing?
- Does the location of the sign warrant renting the sign on an individual basis?

If the sign has clearly been rented as part of a showing, the typical showing for the company must be investigated.

Company rate books in which showings are listed indicate the percentage of the market the showing covers. The rate book will specify the number of poster panels involved in the showing and the number of illuminated and unilluminated signs necessary to cover 25%, 50%, or 100% of the market.

By reviewing the records, the appraiser can ascertain how the poster panel was rented and with what group. The subject sign may have been rented on an individual basis or be listed with a typical number 25 showing, which provides 25% market coverage. Upon investigation the appraiser may find that the typical plant showing is a number 50, indicating 50% market coverage. A historical review of the subject sign may indicate that the sign has been sold with a showing; it may have also been sold at one time with other showings.

If the sign has the potential to be rented on an individual basis sometimes, and as part of a showing at other times, it will be necessary to consider the sign as part of a typical company showing. In this company a number 50 showing may be the typical rental. Since the appraiser is estimating the *most likely* rental for the subject sign, the sign should be considered in the way it will most likely be rented.

ESTIMATING INCOME
An Example

The following exhibit shows the locations of the signs that make up a typical number 100 showing. The showing depicted includes 18 poster panels—12 unilluminated and six illuminated. A 100 showing assumes 100% of the market is covered each day.

Exhibit 7.1 Typical Number 100 Showing—Panel Distribution

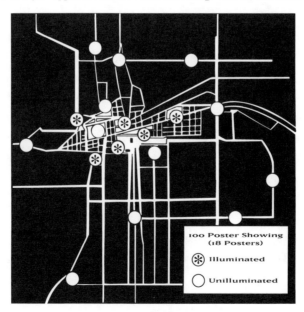

To estimate the income attributable to an individual poster panel in a showing, the appraiser lists all the signs in the showing and the income received. For this number 100 showing, the appraiser would list all 18 signs and their locations. The rental income attributable to the signs would be cited as a gross dollar figure; it would not be allocated among the individual poster panels. In most cases it is quite obvious that the signs do not contribute equally to the gross income generated.

The value and income potential of each sign in the showing will vary based on the visibility of the sign, the daily effective circulation*, and the quality of the circulation.

- The visibility of the sign

  A sign may be well-located, but due to the travel pattern along the highway a driver may pass the sign too quickly to read the copy displayed.
- Daily effective circulation

  Daily effective circulation (DEC) refers to the number of persons who pass the signboard location in a 24-hour period.
- Quality of the circulation

  A sign may be extremely well-located in terms of the number of persons viewing it, but the market may not be one that the advertiser wants to target. The demographics of the area may not be suitable for the product or service the advertiser is promoting.

A sign may be extremely well-located in terms of the number of persons viewing it, but the market may not be one that the advertiser wants to target. The demographics of the area may not be suitable for the product or service the advertiser is promoting.

In the sample 18-poster panel showing, all of the panels do not have the same degree of locational desirability. When the panels are rented to advertisers, there will be considerable variation between the number one location and the number 18 location. To estimate the amount of income generated by a specific sign, all the panels in the showing must be rated. With the rating system, gross income can be allocated based on the income potential of each sign.

Rating Techniques

A showing can be rated by 1) averaging the income, 2) differentiating between illuminated and unilluminated signs, or 3) using daily effective circulation (DEC) data.

* Daily effective circulation (DEC) is rated by the Traffic Audit Bureau. Further information on the Outdoor Visibility Rating System is included in the appendices.

- Averaging the income

  Averaging gross income among the number of signs in a showing is probably the least effective way of measuring the income generated by a sign. To apply this technique, the appraiser divides the gross income by the total number of signs in the showing and multiplies the resulting figure by an appropriate gross income multiplier. There may be occasions when a lack of information forces the appraiser to use this technique but, by and large, this method fails to consider the individual attributes of each sign.

- Illuminated vs. unilluminated

  Obviously an illuminated sign has greater income potential than an unilluminated sign. Were it not for the fact that most signs in urban areas are illuminated, this distinction would be a simple criterion for rating showings. In the 18-sign example, the six illuminated signs probably contribute more to the showing than the 12 unilluminated signs. Therefore, some differentiation between illuminated and unilluminated signs should be made.

- Daily effective circulation (DEC)

  As a third alternative, the appraiser can study daily effective circulation data which track the number of persons who pass the sign. At present this seems to be the most desirable way to rate signs within a showing.

To use daily effective circulation data to rate the 18 posters in the sample showing, the appraiser would first prepare a list showing the location and circulation rating of each sign. Such a list is shown in Exhibit 7.2.

Exhibit 7.2 Poster Panel Locations and DEC Ratings

Panel No.	Location (Street Intersection)	Circulation (in Thousands of Viewers)	Percentage of Total
1	Archer and 33rd Street	25	.099
2	Canal and Van Buren Avenue	10	.040
3	Chicago and Kenton	8	.032
4	Grand and Fairbanks	19	.075
5	Grand and Sayre	13	.052
6	Indiana and 35th Street	33	.131
7	Jefferson and Lexington	6	.024

Panel No.	Location (Street Intersection)	Circulation (in Thousands of Viewers)	Percentage of Total
8	Kedzie and 26th Street	12	.048
9	Laramie and Grand	8	.032
10	Madison and Cicero	17	.067
11	Lasalle and Illinois	24	.095
12	Lake and Ontarioville	3	.012
13	Main and Jackson	4	.016
14	North and Mayfield	18	.071
15	Ogden and Kirkland	10	.040
16	Post and Lowe	4	.016
17	Warrenville and Ivanhoe	4	.016
18	Western and 40th Street	34	.135
		252	1.00

Sign No. 1, which is located at Archer and 33rd Street, has a circulation of 25,000 viewers per day. This figure represents approximately 10% of the 252,000 viewers exposed to the entire showing. Sign No. 5 has a circulation of 13,000, and thus contributes approximately 5% of the viewers to this showing. Using the circulation figures, a percentage breakdown can be established and related to gross income. To derive an estimate of the income generated by an individual sign, the percentage of circulation for that sign is applied to the gross income for the entire showing. Thus it is assumed that Sign No. 5, which contributes 5% of the viewers also contributes 5% of the income to the showing.

In addition to the three methods described above, other methods can be used to rate a showing. The appraiser may consider the combination of a number of factors, including the daily effective circulation (DEC), the position of the sign in the showing, the zoning of the sign site (legally conforming or nonconforming), and the type of signboard construction. All of these factors should be considered in rating a showing.

RATIONALE FOR RATING A SHOWING

The locations and advertising potentials of signs are not equal. Rating a showing is an attempt to measure the advertising potential of individual signs, specifically how location and quality affect a sign's ability to generate income. The rating system is designed to isolate the income of each sign in the showing.

A showing must be rated to estimate the market rent of each specific sign. Once the income stream to the subject sign is estimated, it may be capitalized using a gross income multiplier.

TRAFFIC AUDIT BUREAU INFORMATION

he Traffic Audit Bureau (TAB) for Media Measurement, Inc. is the national authority on out-of-home media. In 1934 TAB was established as an industry audit bureau by the American Association of Advertising Agencies, the Association of National Advertisers, and the Outdoor Advertising Association of America. The Traffic Audit Bureau has a tripartite membership composed of advertisers, advertising agencies, and out-of-home media companies. Like other industry audit bureaus, the majority of the board members are drawn from advertisers and advertising agencies, with control vested in advertisers who buy signboard space. The Traffic Audit Bureau audits circulation past painted bulletins, 30-sheet posters, 8-sheet posters, bus shelter advertising, and bus bench advertising. The bureau also assigns visibility values to 30-sheet poster panels using a system established by the industry.

The daily effective circulation (DEC) data compiled by the Traffic Audit Bureau includes figures on the adult population (18 years and older) and the total population. These data reflect the exposure of an outdoor advertising structure to directional traffic measured in terms of vehicle occupants. The data on unilluminated displays are compiled for 12-hour periods; data on illuminated displays are gathered for either 18- or 24-hour periods. These data are essential to an understanding of the advertising potential of standard outdoor advertising structures.

The Traffic Audit Bureau considers many factors in the measurement of daily effective circulation. These factors include whether a sign has exposure to one-way or two-way traffic and the current occupancy load of the vehicles. The circulation figures used are obtained from sign company records.

The Traffic Audit Bureau has also established an outdoor visibility rating system (OVRS) for the purchasers of sign copy, which was formerly called *space position value*. Using this system outdoor signboards are rated on the amount of setback from the road and the distance of the sign approaches, the length of time the sign can be viewed, the angle at which the sign is positioned, and various other factors that affect the viewing of advertising copy.

The following pages present information used in the analysis of outdoor advertising signs. Sections of the OVRS manual, *How to Use the AAAA Outdoor Visible Rating System for 30-Sheet Posters,* are included in Appendix A along with three plant operator statement forms used in the industry. This information is applicable to advertising signage, not on-premise signs. Appendix B lists the table of contents from another TAB publication, titled *Standard Procedures for the Circulation Evaluation of Outdoor Advertising.* Information on the vehicle load factor, which is important in measuring sign visibility, and the calculation of daily effective circulation is presented in Appendix C.

APPENDIX A
OUTDOOR VISIBILITY RATING SYSTEM AND PLANT OPERATOR STATEMENTS

Because visibility is so essential to successful out-of-home advertising displays, the American Association of Advertising Agencies has developed a new Outdoor Visibility Rating System (OVRS). This system replaces the Space Position Value System.

The OVRS has been developed with the support of the Outdoor Advertising Association of America and has its full endorsement. The system was implemented in January 1990. All TAB member plants are required to evaluate all their 30-sheet poster panels in accordance with the OVRS.

The OVRS gives plants an added marketing value that will be most important in selling their inventory. Plants can earn bonus point awards that increase their qualitative value.

Eligibility Requirements

Before bonus points can be awarded, it is essential to determine whether or not all panels meet the required AAAA minimum visibility standards.

1. Qualifying panels must be within 150 feet from the center of the approach lane.
2. Qualifying panels must be angled to face traffic.
3. No more than two panel facings can be evaluated under the OVR System.
4. Qualifying panels must have a minimum of five seconds of unobstructed approach time, measured at the posted speed limit.

Detailed Explanation Of AAAA Minimum Visibility Standards

1. Qualifying panels must be within 150 feet from the center of the approach lane. Any panel with more than 150 feet of setback does not qualify. Such panels are called *nonqualifying* and receive no OVR system rating.

   Note: In measuring distances for all purposes, a measuring wheel or another precision device must be used to ensure uniformity and accuracy.

2. Qualifying panels must be angled to traffic. One edge of the panel must be set back six feet or more from the other edge as seen from the line of approach. Parallel panels (panels that are built parallel to the line of traffic) are nonqualifying and receive no OVR rating.

3. No more than two panel facings can be rated under the OVR system. Multiple facings of three or more panels are nonqualifying. None of the panels receives a rating. Panels are classified as multiple facings if the panels are within 25 feet of each other.

   Note: Adjacent bulletins, painted walls, junior posters, and other signage are taken into account and treated as panels when rating multiple facings.

4. Qualifying panels must have a minimum of five seconds of clearly visible approach time at the posted speed limit. If obstructions occur within the visible approach either horizontally or vertically, only the unobstructed visible approach time can be counted.

Nonqualifying panels

Panels not meeting one or more of the AAAA minimum visibility standards are called *nonqualifying*. The circulation of such nonqualifying panels will, however, be counted in calculating the plant's average daily effective circulation (DEC).

Awarding Bonus Points

Each panel meeting all minimum visibility standards receives a base OVR of 10.

- Four bonus points are awarded a single panel facing. A panel is classified as single if it is 25 feet away from another panel along the line of traffic or 50 feet away from a bulletin.
- Two bonus points are awarded to panels having a setback of 50 feet or less measured from the middle of the traffic approach lane to the edge of the panel closest to the street.
- Two bonus points are awarded to the street-end panel in a two-panel facing. The street-end panel is the one closest to the line of traffic. The panel farthest from the traffic is the inside panel. The inside panel meets the minimum visibility standards, but does not get any bonus points.
- Two bonus points are awarded to any panel in the immediate vicinity of any of the following features: a stop sign, a toll booth, a flashing red indicator. A panel is in the immediate vicinity if it is within 250 feet before or after the feature in the approach lane to or away from the panel.
- One bonus point is awarded to any panel in the immediate vicinity of a traffic light or flashing yellow indicator.
- One bonus point is awarded to the upper and lower panel on a stacked panel structure. Each panel receives one bonus point.
- One bonus point is awarded to a panel with 51 to 100 feet of setback.
- One bonus point is awarded for each additional second of approach time beyond the minimum five seconds needed to qualify.

Procedure

First, note the posted speed limit for the area where the panel is located. Next, measure the distance from the panel to the point where the panel first becomes visible. Then, accurately measure the distance from that point to the point where the panel passes out of sight, disregarding any distance during which the view of the panel is obstructed.

Measuring the approach distance for two-panel facings will sometimes require riding the location twice—once for the street-end panel and again for the inside panel. In some instances, the approach distances will be different.

Using the posted speed limit and the approach distance, the TAB Approach Table can be used to obtain the seconds of approach time—i.e., the amount of time the sign is visible to passing traffic. To calculate the bonus points, subtract the five seconds of minimum approach time from the total approach time.

After calculating the applicable bonus points, this figure is added to the base of 10 for qualifying panels. The total is recorded along with the proper code designation. The OVRS code designations are:

S   Single panel

E   Street-end panel in a two-panel facing

A   Inside panel in a two-panel facing

U   Upper panel in a stacked location

L   Lower panel in a stacked location

P   Parallel panel

M   Multiple panel (three or more in a facing)

The total OVRS is divided by the total number of panels in the market to get the average OVR for the market. The average OVR is recorded on the plant operator statement, which is distributed to the plant, member agencies, and advertisers.

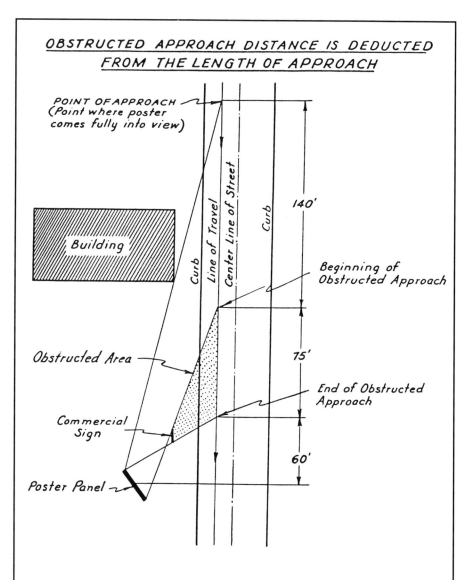

OBSTRUCTED APPROACH DISTANCE IS DEDUCTED FROM THE LENGTH OF APPROACH

TOTAL APPROACH DISTANCE (140' + 75' + 60') = 275'

LESS TOTAL OBSTRUCTED APPROACH DISTANCE = 75'

TOTAL UNOBSTRUCTED APPROACH DISTANCE = 200'

TAB Approach Time Conversion Table

Distance required to see poster panel for:

At Speed	5 SEC.	6 SEC.	7 SEC.	8 SEC.	9 SEC.	10 SEC.
15 mph	110	132	154	176	198	221
20 mph	147	176	206	235	265	294
25 mph	184	221	257	294	331	368
30 mph	221	265	309	353	397	441
35 mph	257	309	360	412	463	515
40 mph	294	353	412	470	529	588
45 mph	331	397	463	529	595	662
50 mph	368	441	515	588	662	735
55 mph	404	485	566	647	728	809
60 mph	441	529	617	706	794	882
65 mph	478	573	669	764	860	956
Additional points		1	2	3	4	5

TAB AUDITED
PLANT OPERATOR STATEMENT
BULLETINS

AUTHENTICATED CIRCULATION OF OUT-OF-HOME ADVERTISING

1. MARKET

2. STATE   AUDIT DATE

3. BULLETIN OPERATOR AUDITED:

NOTES TO BUYER:

4. OTHER AUDITED BULLETIN OPERATOR(S) IN MARKET:
(See their respective TAB Audit Statements.)

	Size	Number	Estimated Avg. DEC*
Total Audited Rotating Bulletins as of above date:			

	Size	Number
Total Audited Permanent Bulletins as of above date:		

DEC Range of Rotaries

DEC	NUMBER	%
under 10,000		
10,000-19,999		
20,000-29,999		
30,000+		

*Caution: Be advised that the estimated average DEC is based on the Rotary Plan as of the time of audit. This average may vary over the three year audit cycle due to the interchange ability of the Rotary and Permanent classifications.

Contact the Plant Operator for:
— The TAB individually audited, signed and stamped statement for each location.
— The current average DEC as it pertains to presently available Rotating Bulletins.

Morning Illumination note:

CERTIFICATION STATEMENT:
The records maintained by the company audited shown on this report have been examined by the Traffic Audit Bureau for Media Measurement, Inc. The examination was made in accordance with auditing procedures generally employed by the Traffic Audit Bureau for Media Measurement, Inc. and accordingly include such tests of the records and other such auditing prodecures as considered necessary under the circumstances. Based on our examination, the data on this report present fairly the information relating to the bulletins of this market as verified by our auditor.

DATE _____

THE TRAFFIC AUDIT BUREAU FOR MEDIA MEASUREMENT, INC

TRAFFIC AUDIT BUREAU FOR MEDIA MEASUREMENT, INC.
114 EAST 32nd STREET · NEW YORK, N.Y. 10016 · PHONE (212) 213-9640 · FAX (212) 889-4092

President

AUTHENTICATED CIRCULATION OF OUT-OF-HOME ADVERTISING

TAB

AUDITED

PLANT OPERATOR STATEMENT

EIGHT-SHEET POSTERS

1. MARKET

2. STATE   AUDIT DATE

3. AUDITED PLANT OPERATOR:

4. OTHER TAB MEMBER PLANT(S) IN MARKET:
(See their respective TAB Audit Statements.)

5. MARKET AREA SERVED:

Counties	Pop. (000)	# Panels	Average DEC* Per Panel	Average Space Position Value

TOTALS:

6.

MAJOR CITIES	# Panels	Total Pop. (000)	Black Pop. (000)	Hispanic Pop. (000)

7. PANEL PROFILE:

%

Single

Multiple

8. NOTES:

*AVERAGE DAILY EFFECTIVE CIRCULATION PER PANEL:
Illuminated: 24 hours
                18 hours 6 a.m.–midnight
Unilluminated: 12 hours 6 a.m.–6 p.m.

9. CIRCULATION SOURCES:

% Manual   % Official

10. AGE OF CIRCULATION DATA:

% Under 3 years   % Over 3 years

TRAFFIC AUDIT BUREAU FOR MEDIA MEASUREMENT, INC.
114 EAST 32nd STREET · NEW YORK, N.Y. 10016 · PHONE (212) 213-9640 · FAX (212) 889-4092

AUTHENTICATED CIRCULATION OF OUT-OF-HOME ADVERTISING

TAB
AUDITED
PLANT OPERATOR STATEMENT
SHELTER ADVERTISING

1. MARKET

2. STATE   AUDIT DATE

3. AUDITED PLANT OPERATOR:

4. OTHER TAB MEMBER PLANT(S) IN MARKET:
   (See their respective TAB Audit Statements.)

5. MARKET AREA SERVED:

Counties	Pop. (000)	# Panels	Average DEC* Per Panel

TOTALS:

6.

MAJOR CITIES	# Panels	Total Pop. (000)	Black Pop. (000)	Hispanic Pop. (000)

7. CIRCULATION SOURCES:

% Manual   % Official

8. AGE OF CIRCULATION DATA:

% Under 3 years   % Over 3 years

9. NOTES:

*AVERAGE DAILY EFFECTIVE CIRCULATION PER PANEL: Illuminated: 24 hours,18 hours 6 a.m.–midnight. Unilluminated: 12 hours 6 a.m.-6 p.m.

TRAFFIC AUDIT BUREAU FOR MEDIA MEASUREMENT, INC.
114 EAST 32nd STREET · NEW YORK, N.Y. 10016 · PHONE (212) 213-9640 · FAX (212) 889-4092

APPENDIX B
STANDARD PROCEDURE
FOR EVALUATING THE CIRCULATION OF
OUTDOOR ADVERTISING

The following pages present the full table of contents from *Standard Procedure for the Circulation Evaluation of Outdoor Advertising,* eighth edition, published by the Traffic Audit Bureau.

PART ONE **PLANT OPERATOR'S AREAS OF RESPONSIBILITY** I

Chapter I 2-15

Rule 1- Records to be Installed 2-6

Information Required 3

Examples of Numbering System 4-6

Rule 2- What is a Completed Advertising Structure 8

Rule 3- What is to be Audited? 8

Rule 4- What is Not to be Audited? 8

Detailed Instructions on How to Use TAB

Forms 11, 12, and 14 9-15

Chapter II **16-25**

Methods of Collecting Traffic Data 16

Rule 1 - The Plant Operator is Responsible for Obtaining All

           Traffic Data 16

Rule 2 - Counting Stations Must be Established Along All the

           Routes of Travel in Each Market Where Advertising

           Structures are Located 16

Rule 3 - Each Counting Station Must be Assigned a Number 17

Rule 4 - Each Counting Station Must Show Where the

           Count was Made 19

Rule 5 - The Traffic Counting Station Must Reflect the Volume

           of Traffic Passing the Advertising Structures 19

Rule 6 - Methods of Reporting Traffic Count Data 19-25

           Machine Traffic Data 19-21

           Accuracy Limits of Average Daily Traffic 20

           How to Obtain Circulation From Traffic Volume Obtained by

           Machine Counts 21

           Hand Counting Must Follow Procedures 23-24

           How to Obtain Circulation From Traffic Volume Obtained by

           Hand Counts 25

Chapter III **26-30**

Means to Establish Index of Visibility (Space Position Value) 26-30

Rule 1 - All Standard Poster Panels Must be Rated and

           Assigned a Code 26

            Form D - Space Position Value Table 27

Rule 2 - Advertising Structures Not up to AAAA Standards, if Sold,

           Must be Clearly Marked Non-AAAA Standard 28

Rule 3 - The Approach Distance Applicable to an Advertising Structure

           is the Distance Measured Along the Line of Travel From the

           Point the Panel Becomes Fully Visible to the Point at Which

           the Traffic Stream Passes By the Center of the Panel 28

Rule 4 - The Maximum Visibility Limit of a Poster Panel is Set

           at 500 Feet 28

Rule 5- Slow Traffic is Defined as All Arterials Where Posted Speeds are Not Over 35 MPH. Fast Traffic is Defined as All Arterials Where Posted Speeds are Over 35 MPH 28

Rule 6- Setback Reductions Must be Applied to Panels 28

Rule 7- The Primary SPV is Established by the Street Which has the Highest Circulation When a Panel May be Seen From Two or More Streets. All Other SPVs Other Than the Primary are Recorded in the Secondary SPV Rating Column on Form 11 28

Rule 8- SPV Ratings Should Reflect the Average Lane Used by Traffic 29

Rule 9- Minimum Secondary SPVs That May be Assigned: No Values Lower Than a Grade of 5 May be Used 29

Rule 10-Where a Panel has More Than a Short Approach From Two Directions and is Not a Parallel Panel, Use the Total Street Circulation 29

Rule 11-Angled Panels are Advertising Structures Built so That Maximum Visibility Will be to Vehicles Approaching the Structure. Advertising Structures are Classified as Angled When One End is More Than 6 Feet Back From the Other End 29

Rule 12-A Panel is Classified as Single if it is 25' Away From Another Panel Along the Line of Travel or 50' Away From a Bulletin 29

Rule 13-The Poster Nearest to the Street is Classified as an "AE" in a Multiple Panel Facing or in a Single Panel, an "AS". Panels Adjacent to an "AE" are Classified "A" if Angled. A Parallel Panel is Classified as "PS" if a Single Structure. Parallel Panels of Multiple Facing Will be Classified as "P" 23

Rule 14-Panels Vertically Built (Decked) Will be Coded So That the Lower is "AE", Upper is "A" With the Distance Coded According to Length of Approach 29

Rule 15- Approach Distance for Parallel Panels Should be Applied
        as Defined in This Rule. 30

Rule 16-The Circulation That Can be Applied for Parallel Panels
        Can Only be One-Half the Total Circulation on the Street ... 30

Rule 17- Situations Not Covered in This Chapter Must be Referred
        to TAB for Ruling 30

PART TWO –**TRAFFIC AUDIT BUREAU'S AUDITING PROCEDURE AND**
    PUBLICATIONS **31**

Chapter IV **32-36**
    General Procedure for Auditing 32
    Determination of Clerical Accuracy 33
    Sample Selection for Field Audit 34
    Auditing Procedures 35
    Analysis and Preparation of Audit Data for Publication 36

Chapter V **37-42**
    Plant Operator's Statement and Rules Governing Publication
    With Examples 37-42

APPENDIX C
VEHICLE LOAD FACTOR AND DAILY
EFFECTIVE CIRCULATION

The material on the following pages was extracted from two TAB publications: *Addressing the Importance of the Vehicle Load Factor and its Effect on the Measurement of Out-of-Home Media* and *Factors for Calculating Daily Effective Circulation.*

New Vehicle Load Factor to Refine Out-of-Home Audience Data

Over the years, the Traffic Audit Bureau has worked to improve the methodology of measuring exposure to out-of-home advertising. This effort has resulted in the new 15-minute counting methodology, more information on plant operator statements, and visibility standards.

Adjusting the outdated *vehicle load factor is* the latest TAB refinement.

The vehicle load factor is the average number of people per vehicle and is an integral part of calculating Daily Effective Circulation or *DEC* (i.e., the number of advertising exposures generated each day).

Since 1937, a load factor of 1.75 persons per car has been standard. Obviously, this number is now outdated, as evidenced by the increase in car ownership and changes in the demographics and traffic patterns of the U.S. consumer. For example:

- According to the U.S. Census, between 1960 and 1988 motor vehicle registrations increased by 148 percent while population increased by only 36 percent.
- During the same period, women in the work force increased from 38 percent to 45 percent, adding more vehicles per household.
- The latest Federal Highway Administration survey shows that, as of 1990, over 60 percent of all households now have two or more vehicles.
- As population shifts have continued from cities to suburbs, lack of public transportation has caused more individual use of cars.

It is clear from these facts that average vehicle occupancy is trending downward. Therefore, TAB sponsored extensive national research to study the load factor issue and concluded that the present load factor should be adjusted.

Special questions were included in the two most widely used national consumer behavior surveys, *Simmons Market Research Bureau* (SMRB) and *Mediamark Research, Inc.* (MRI). The questions asked respondents about their last trip in a car. The survey results were then checked against a separate nationwide field observation study undertaken by *Market Information Services of America* (MISA), a professional traffic engineering firm. The field observations were conducted to verify the accuracy of the SMRB and MRI surveys.

The correlation between the three sources reinforces their consistency and reliability:

		Average Vehicle Occupancy
SMRB (20,000 interviews)	Adults 18+	1.35
MRI (10,000 interviews)	Adults 18+	1.36
MISA (10,000 field observations)	Adults 18+	1.36
MISA (10,000 field observations)	All occupants	1.46

TAB selected the SMRB results of 1.35 to serve as the official average occupancy figure. Using the SMRB data not only allows TAB to include the vehicle occupancy question in SMRB's future surveys, but also supports the ability to aggregate data over subsequent years. This offers the potential of more definitive vehicle load factors or even of regional load factors.

TAB also chose to base audited circulation on adults 18+ to be comparable with other media audience data.

New Vehicle Load Factor Based on Adult Data

A major goal of our industry has been to facilitate agency and advertising media planning by making out-of-home audience data directly comparable to the data supplied by other media.

Effective January 1, 1992, the new adults 18+ vehicle load factor of 1.35, combined with the new adults 18+ population base, accomplishes this. Previously, the load factor of 1.75 persons per vehicle was based on total audience.

The industry's new Harris Donovan outdoor planning system for audience reach and frequency by market will utilize TAB circulation data based on the new 1.35 adults 18+ vehicle load factor; reach and frequency data for most out-of-home media will be anchored to TAB-audited circulation of the 18+ population by market; all corollary data available from the SMRB consumer survey will be based on the 18+ audience. Thus, all out-of-home audience data will be based on the same adult 18+ audience system.

Presenting out-of-home audience data in formats comparable to other media audience data will increase top-of-mind awareness among media planners. Out-of-home data will be more accurate, more credible, and easier to use.

Effect on plant allotments

While providing the aforementioned benefits for media planning, the effects on allotments will be minimal. As plant managers move to an adult 18+ daily effective circulation base, they will also move to an adult 18+ population universe for their allotments. When calculating the GRPs per showings, each plant operator must allocate panels based on adult 18+ DECs applied against the adult 18+ population.

The national average population of adults 18+ is 74.6% of the total population. The new 18+ vehicle load factor of 1.35 persons per vehicle is 77.1% of the old load factor of 1.75. Thus, the gap between these two percentages will result in only a slight drop in allotments in most markets. This is illustrated as follows.

Market X

Total market population: 1,750,000

Circulation before load factor is applied: 10,000

Using old load factor

Average DEC:

10,000 X 1.75 = 17,500

(Circulation) x (old load factor) = DEC

Number of panels required to deliver 100 daily GRPs = 100

17,500 X 100 = 1,750,000

(DEC) x (panels) = (Total market population)

Using new load factor

Converting to adults 18+ population base and utilizing new adult 18+ vehicle load factor:

(Total population) x (% adults 18+) = adults

1,750,000 X 74.6% = 1,305,000

Revised DEC:

10,000 X 1.35 = 13,500

(Circulation) x (new load factor) = DEC

Number of panels required to deliver 100 daily GRPs = 97

13,500 X 97 = 1,309,500

(DEC) x (panels) = (Adult 18+ population)

Number of panels needed for 100 GRPs:

Total population base = 100

Adult 18+ population base = 97

Percent reduction in number of panels needed = 3%

By comparison, if TAB were to continue to base circulation on total vehicle occupants, instead of adults 18+, there would be a much greater effect on allotments. The old
load factor of 1.75 (total occupants) would be reduced to 1.46 (total occupants), as
determined by field research. This would have resulted in a reduction in circulation of
nearly 17%, *without* any corresponding reduction in population. In this case, current
allotments would be *under-delivering by 17%.*

*This illustrates that there is a definite operational benefit as well as a marketing
benefit in using an adult 18+population and circulation base. The effect on allotments is
minimal.*

Effective data for new load factor is January 1992

As approved at the recent TAB Board meeting, the new load factor will become effective
January 1, 1992. After that date, all TAB audits will be based on the new load factor,
including the 1989-1991 audits which are already completed.

Audit statement adjustments

All 1992 audits will automatically utilize the new load factor and 18+ population data as
the audits occur. Audit results for the years 1989-1991 will be adjusted to reflect the new
load factor and adult 18+ population data. TAB will distribute to the plant the adjusted
DEC which in all cases will be 77.1% of the old DEC. In the same document, TAB will provide
the adult 18+ population for the market. The plant will then have the choice of using TAB
data or providing its own.

TAB will notify advertisers and advertising agencies of the new population and DEC
data for all markets. A list of all TAB audited markets over 25,000 population will be
distributed to the buying community in September 1991. The list will contain the adjusted
population base (adults 18+) and adjusted daily effective circulation (adults 18+ DEC).

The process for adjusting 1989-1991 audit population figures will be:

- TAB will secure current county population data for the plant's market(s) from
  accredited sources. This will be sent to the plants very soon.
- The plant will have the option to use these figures to compare their new 18+
  population base or to use their own legitimate source. The source of the latter
  must be furnished to TAB for verification.
- The plant will be asked to respond with this data by a deadline date. If no
  response is received by that date, the market population figure as it appears on

the last plant operator statement will be lowered by 25.4%. This adjustment is based on the national average of adult 18+ population being 74.6% of the total population.

TAB will soon distribute a document explaining this procedure in greater detail. It is important that TAB receive this data promptly to insure that the adjusted DEC and population figures are distributed to the buying community before 1992 planning time begins.

Prompt attention to this will be greatly appreciated.

Where required, plants should adjust their allotments on 1992 rate cards and in the various buyers guides to reflect vehicle load factor changes.

More information to come

TAB will soon distribute a memo containing the new multiplying factors to be applied to official data and hand counts that will have to be used in preparing 1992 audits.

TAB is available to answer questions on this important change.

The Traffic Audit Bureau For Media Measurement

114 E. 32nd Street

New York, NY 10016

212/213-9640

FAX 212/889-4092

Factors for Calculating Daily Effective Circulation

The Traffic Audit Bureau for Media Measurement is the national verification authority for out-of-home media. Established in 1934 as an industry audit bureau by the American Association of Advertising Agencies, the Association of National Advertisers and the Outdoor Advertising Association of America, the TAB now audits circulation to painted bulletins, 10-sheet posters, eight-sheet posters, bus shelter advertising, and bus bench advertising. TAB also audits visibility values of the 30-sheet medium as established by an industry-approved system.

The TAB is tripartite with membership support from advertisers, advertising agencies and out-of-home media companies. Control is vested in the buyers with majority representation on the Board drawn from advertisers and agencies, similar to other industry audit bureaus.

Vehicular circulation

Advertising exposure to out-of-home advertising is called daily effective circulation (DEC). DEC is computed by factors that calibrate period of exposure, directional traffic, and vehicle occupancy. Unilluminated displays are allowed 12 hours of exposure, while illuminated displays are allowed 18 or 24 hours depending on whether the lights are turned off at midnight or daybreak. All two-way traffic is converted into effective directional traffic. The current load factor to determine vehicle occupancy is 1.35. DEC converts traffic counts to people exposure. Traffic counts are derived from two sources: official and manual.

Official counts are generally available from departments of transportation at city, county or state agencies. State counts are taken on most roadways in three-year cycles, while city and other regional agencies provide these data less frequently. Conversion factors for 24-hour traffic data are shown below.

Factors to Convert Official 24-Hour Counts to DEC

Period of Exposure	Factor
24 hours	.675
18 hours	.64
12 hours	.45

Manual counts are performed by the plant operator. The tally method utilizing hand tally counters is recommended. Short counts of 15 minutes in duration are conducted of vehicles between 9 a.m. and noon or 1 p.m. and 4 p.m. There are two sets of factors for converting manual counts to DEC. The first set expands 15 minutes to one hour and the factors vary by time of count. The second, which varies with the period of exposure, is used to expand the one-hour equivalent to DEC. These factors are shown below.

Multiplying Factors for 15-Minute Hand Counts

MORNING			
Starting Time (AM)	MF	Starting Time (AM)	MF
9:00—9:45	5.14	10:00—10:45	4.75
9:46	5.11	10:46	4.70
9:47	5.09	10:47	4.66
9:48	5.06	10:48	4.61
9:49	5.04	10:49	4.56
9:50	5.01	10:50	4.51
9:51	4.98	10:51	4.47
9:52	4.96	10:52	4.42
9:53	4.93	10:53	4.37
9:54	4.91	10:54	4.32
9:55	4.88	10:55	4.28
9:56	4.85	10:56	4.23
9:57	4.83	10:57	4.18
9:58	4.80	10:58	4.13
9:59	4.78	10:59	4.09
		11:00—11:45	4.04

AFTERNOON			
Starting Time (PM)	MF	Starting Time (PM)	MF
1:00—1:45	3.83	2:00—2:45	3.71
1:46	3.82	2:46	3.68
1:47	3.81	2:47	3.65
1:48	3.81	2:48	3.62
1:49	3.80	2:49	3.59
1:50	3.79	2:50	3.56
1:51	3.78	2:51	3.53
1:52	3.77	2:52	3.50
1:53	3.77	2:53	3.47
1:54	3.76	2:54	3.44
1:55	3.75	2:55	3.41
1:56	3.74	2:56	3.38
1:57	3.73	2:57	3.35
1:58	3.73	2:58	3.32
1:59	3.72	2:59	3.29
		3:00—3:45	3.26

Multiplying Factors for Expanding One-Hour Equivalents to DEC

Period of Exposure	Factor
24 hours	10.9
18 hours	10.4
12 hours	7.3

Important: If any count—manual or official—is taken on a one-way street, the factors must be doubled because of the built-in divisor for directional circulation. However, do not ever double the 15-minute multiplying factors nor the base count of the vehicles.

Pedestrian circulation

The present method of calculating pedestrian circulation to out-of-home advertising requires two half-hour counts. These are conducted between 9 a.m. and noon and 1 p.m. and 4 p.m. Two separate half-hour counts are taken for each counting station. The resulting one-hour count is then expanded, as follows:

Period of Exposure	Factor
18 hours	9
12 hours	6

GLOSSARY

The following definitions are presented to help real estate appraisers understand the signboard industry and its terminology.

advertising agency. An independent business organization that creates, prepares, and places advertisements in various media for its clients.

A frame. A type of sign structure supported by an A-shaped back brace.

agency commission. A fee paid to an advertising agency by a plant operator for placing business (leasing space) with the plant operator.

allotment. The number of unilluminated and illuminated panels in a showing.

American Council of Highway Advertisers (ACHA). A trade association which represents highway advertisers; located in North Beach, Maryland.

amortization. An accounting term used to describe the process of depreciating an asset over a period of time. In relation to billboards, *amortization* describes a grace period between the time a sign owner is notified that the sign must be removed and the time when the sign is actually removed. A process relating to the taking of signs without compensation.

animation. A technique used on bulletins to activate one or more moving parts.

approach. Distance from which an outdoor advertising structure is clearly visible; measured in feet.

apron. The decorative trim beneath the bottom molding of a sign; usually found on painted bulletins; synonymous with *base*.

availability. The number of poster panels available for sale on any given posting date.

back to back. Two or more outdoor advertising sign panels that are erected on one structure and face in opposite directions.

base. The decorative trim beneath the bottom molding of a sign; usually found on painted bulletins; synonymous with *apron*.

bill. A poster.

billboard. A panel or flat surface, usually outdoors, for displaying notices or advertisements. Commonly, standardized wooden or steel structures that carry either poster paper or painted messages.

blanking paper. White paper used around advertising display copy to form a border between the poster and the panel molding.

bleed posting. The use of blanking paper the same color as the poster background to bring the design display area up to the inside panel molding.

block. An object that obstructs the view of an advertising structure.

boards. A common term for poster panels and painted bulletins.

booked. Describes a poster plant in which every poster panel is sold to an advertiser by a given posting date.

bottom molding. The lower edge of an outdoor advertising structure.

bulletins. Very large advertising structures, usually 14 feet x 48 feet or 10 feet, 6 inches x 36 feet. The design is painted directly on the surface and a preprinted advertising message is affixed. When painting is the method of reproduction, the bulletin is called a *paint* or *painted bulletin*.

bundle of rights theory. A concept that compares property ownership to a bundle of sticks with each stick representing a distinct and separate right of the property owner— e.g., the right to use real estate, to sell it, to lease it, to give it away, or to choose to exercise all or none of these rights.

buy. Within the sign industry, the leasing of sign space.

buyer. Within the sign industry, the renter of a sign, i.e., the advertiser. See also *sale*.

cancellation period. The period during which posting contracts may be cancelled; usually the sign company must be notified 60 to 90 days before the posting date.

cans. Incandescent light fixtures attached to an illuminated outdoor advertising structure; synonymous with *reflector shades*.

cantilever construction. A type of sign construction used to prevent various types of trespassing. The sign face is set off from the supporting beams.

checking. The inspection of outdoor advertising structures and analysis of their maintenance.

circulation. Number of potential viewers, which forms the foundation for determining the advertising value of out-of-home media. Outdoor circulation is based on traffic volume, which is made up of automotive, pedestrian, and mass transportation.

collating. Arranging the individual sheets of a poster in the sequence in which they will be posted.

commercial sign. Any sign that advertises a product, service, entertainment, or commodity sold or offered on the premises where the sign is located; often referred to as a *business sign* or *identification sign*; synonymous with *identification*.

competitive plants. Two or more outdoor plants operating in the same market.

conforming sign. A sign that was legally erected in accordance with the federal, state and local laws in effect at the time of its erection.

cooperative outdoor advertising. An arrangement in which the manufacturer and distributor or dealer of a product or service share in the cost of a sign.

copy. The pictorial design, background, word copy, and message to be displayed on a poster panel or painted bulletin.

cost approach. A valuation approach in which the appraiser determines the replacement cost of an improvement, subtracts any accrued depreciation, and adds land value to estimate the value of a real property.

coverage. A marketing term that designates the area, group, or consumer segment that is to be exposed to outdoor advertising.

customized rotation. Painted bulletins that are moved to new locations in the market on specific dates and tailored to the clients' particular needs.

custom-made posters. Hand-painted, lithographed, or screen-processed posters made in small quantities for use principally by local merchants in markets with populations under 100,000.

cutouts and extensions. Plywood reproductions of copy, e.g., figures, cars, other attention-getting graphics placed on painted bulletins to emphasize the copy or advertising message; synonymous with *embellishments*.

date strips. Sheets announcing the date of an advertised event, usually pasted over an existing poster. *See also* overlay; snipe.

daily effective circulation (DEC). Average number of persons 18 years and older exposed each day to a sign or group of signs; measured for a 12- hour period for unilluminated signs and for an 18-hour period for illuminated signs. *See also* circulation.

design. The artwork and text that make up a poster or painted bulletin.

directional signs. Signs designed to help people locate restaurants, lodging, local attractions, real estate development, etc.

display. A sign structure that shows a single advertising message.

display period. The time when outdoor advertising copy is on display.

district showing. Poster panels placed in a portion of a market as opposed to full market coverage.

double deck. Two or more poster panels, one set higher than the other.

effective circulation. *See* circulation; daily effective circulation.

effective gross income *(EGI).* The anticipated income from the operation of real property, adjusted for vacancy and collection losses.

eight-sheet panel. A 72-sq.-ft. poster panel generally placed for exposure to pedestrian as well as vehicular traffic; found predominately in urban areas.

embellishment. Any added sign feature such as a bulletin cutout, neon or plastic letters, clocks, and electrical devices. *See also* cutouts and extensions.

face. The panel surface of the sign that carries the advertising message.

facing. The direction in which panels are positioned to display the advertising copy; e.g., a south-facing panel can be read by northbound traffic.

fee simple estate. Absolute ownership unencumbered by any other interest or estate, subject only to the four powers of government.

flagged or flagging. A poster that is torn, waving, or hanging from the face of the panel.

flank. A poster panel that is on the same horizontal level as another poster panel and faces the same direction.

frequency. The approximate number of times a poster panel will be viewed in a given period of time.

gross rent multiplier (GRM). The relationship or ratio between sale price or value and gross rental income.

hand-painted posters. Posters manufactured individually, usually for local advertisers who need only a small number or want them produced very quickly.

head-on. A location directly in front of approaching traffic, usually at the beginning or end of a curve in the road.

high-spot. A rooftop location, frequently used in congested areas.

highway bulletin. A painted outdoor advertising sign approximately 12 feet x 40 feet, located in a rural area, and usually featuring permanent copy.

highway wall. An advertisement painted directly on the side of a building along a main highway which can be viewed by passing traffic.

identification sign. *See* commercial sign.

illegal sign. A sign that is erected or maintained in violation of state or local laws.

illuminated panel. A panel with strong overhead lights that shine directly on the copy; usually located on streets with heavy night traffic. Illumination is provided from dusk until midnight in most cases.

imprint. The name of the owner of the sign structure, which is usually found on the top or bottom molding of the sign.

incandescent. A type of brilliant illumination produced when a filament within the lamp is heated by electricity.

income approach. A valuation approach based on analyzing the amount of net income a property will produce over its remaining economic life.

intensive showing. A showing that consists of either one and one-half or two times as many poster panels as a representative showing; used to provide intensified repetition and market coverage.

Institute of Outdoor Advertising (IOA). The marketing information and creative center for the Outdoor Advertising Association of America (OAAA). The Institute provides in-depth marketing materials as well as training and support to OAAA members, advertisers, and their agencies. It also serves as the communications link between OAAA members and the advertising community and conducts marketing and creative seminars.

larger parcel. In condemnation the portion of a property that has unity of ownership, contiguity, and unity of use, the three conditions that establish the larger parcel for the consideration of severance damages in most states. Sometimes contiguity is subordinated to unity of use. Used synonymously with *parent holding*.

lease. Contract covering the rental of the land on which painted bulletins or poster panels are erected.

leasehold estate. The right to use and occupy real estate for a stated term and under certain conditions; conveyed by a lease.

leasehold improvements. Improvements or additions to leased property that have been made by the lessee.

lease interest. One of the real property interests that results from the separation of the bundle of rights by a lease, i.e., the leased fee estate or the leasehold estate.

legal nonconforming use. A use that was lawfully established, but no longer conforms to the use regulations of the zone in which it is located.

length of approach. The distance from which a painted bulletin or poster panel is clearly visible; measured in feet.

lithography. A method of printing used in the mass production of posters. The design to be reproduced is etched on metal plates and the plates are inked and put under pressure, transferring the design to paper. This is the method most often employed in the production of posters.

load factor. The number of passengers per vehicle.

location list. List of sign locations where advertisers' copy is to appear during a specified time period.

long side. A panel on the left side of the street facing traffic on the right side of the street; sometimes called *left-hand reader* or *cross-traffic location*.

maintenance. The cleaning, painting, repair, or replacement of defective parts of billboards in a manner that does not alter the basic copy, design, or structure of the sign.

market value. The major focus of most real property appraisal assignments. Economic and legal definitions of market value have been developed and refined. The market value concept is essential to the appraisal profession. The following definition of market value is widely accepted by real estate appraisers:

The most probable price, as of a specified date, in cash, or in terms equivalent to cash, or in other precisely revealed terms, for which the specified property rights should sell after reasonable exposure in a competitive market under all conditions requisite to a fair sale, with the buyer and seller each acting prudently, knowledgeably, and for self-interest, and assuming that neither is under undue duress. (*The Appraisal of Real Estate,* 10th ed., published in 1992 by the Appraisal Institute.)

Many legal definitions of market value are based on the following:

The highest price estimated in terms of money that the land would bring if exposed for sale in the open market, with reasonable time allowed in which to find a purchaser, buying with knowledge of all of the uses and purposes to which it was adapted, and for which it was capable of being used. [*Sacramento Southern R.R. Co.* v. *Heilbron* 156 Cal. 408, 104 p. 979 (1909).]

Individuals performing appraisal services that may be subject to litigation are cautioned to seek the exact definition of market value in the jurisdiction in which the services are being performed. For further discussion of this important term, see *The Appraisal of Real Estate,* 10th ed., pp. 18-22.

metropolitan highway and railroad bulletin. An extra-large painted display bulletin located along a highway or transportation line approaching a metropolitan center; has a standard overall size of 18 feet x 72 feet.

minimum showing. A showing of half as many panels as a representative showing; used in a few cases to keep a limited advertising campaign active.

molding. The frame of a painted bulletin or poster panel.

multivision. An embellishment measuring 18 feet, 9 inches x 16 feet, 10 inches with a display area of 16 feet x 16 feet, which is affixed to the face of a painted bulletin. The unit consists of 16 vertical, triangular louvers which revolve at regular intervals, delivering three distinct advertising messages; synonymous with *trivision.*

NAC rating. Net advertising circulation rating. This figure results from multiplying the space position value (SPV) by the daily effective circulation (DEC). The NAC of all structures in a plant many be summed to yield a total NAC for the entire plant; then the proportionate contribution of each structure can be calculated.

neighborhood showing. Coverage of one or more neighborhood shopping districts by outdoor advertising.

neon. Luminous tubing used for advertising; visible both night and day.

noncompete agreement. An agreement in a sales document which restricts the seller from competing with the purchaser by constructing new signs or leasing sign space; usually relates to a specific time period and a specific area.

occupancy factor. The ratio between the income derived from the rental units currently occupied and the income that would be derived if all the units were occupied.

official sign. Directional signs and other notices erected and maintained by public officials or agencies pursuant to and in accordance with the directions or authorizations contained in state or federal laws.

on-premise signs. Signs that are not part of the standardized industry since, by definition, the space on these signs is not for rent. This type of sign carries the message of the business or service that owns it and on whose property it is usually located.

opaque printing. A printing process which usually employs a series of screens, layering one color over other colors without losing any of the value of the top color; does not permit the blending of colors.

outdoor advertising. A general term which covers any form of outdoor sign.

Outdoor Advertising Association of America, Inc. (OAAA). An organization that represents the standardized outdoor advertising industry in the United States. Located in Washington, D.C., OAAA is the collective voice of many outdoor advertising companies, operators, suppliers, and affiliates from the United States and abroad. The OAAA provides technical assistance to its members and serves as a clearinghouse for national and regional public service advertising campaigns. In addition, OAAA represents industry interests before Congress and regulatory agencies and also provides assistance to its members as they work with local and state governments.

outdoor advertising industry. Companies that own and maintain signs and rent sign space to advertisers.

Outdoor Visibility Rating System (OVRS). A rating of the visibility of a poster to passing traffic; based on length of approach, speed of travel, angle of panel to circulation, and relationship to adjacent travel.

out-of-home media. Industry term for sign advertising.

overlay. A sheet posted over a section of a poster showing a price, a date, or other timely information; synonymous with *snipe*.

override. The period of time a plant operator allows a poster to remain up after the 30-day leasing period has expired.

package. A group of rented signs.

painted wall. An advertisement painted directly on the wall of a building so that it can be viewed by passing traffic. *See also* highway wall.

paint plant. All of the painted bulletins in a given area owned or operated by one operator.

paper. *See* poster.

parallel. Describes a structure parallel to the flow of traffic.

parent holding. *See* larger parcel.

permanent paint. *See* bulletin.

permit. A license granted by a state or locality which authorizes a sign.

plant. The total number of outdoor structures under a single ownership in a city. *See also* larger parcel.

plant imprint. A wood or metal plate on an advertising structure that identifies the plant operator.

plant operator. The owner or manager of an outdoor advertising company conducting business in a particular city or area.

position. The placement of an outdoor structure on a certain site, i.e., the angle of the unit in relation to the road, height from ground, direction it faces, etc.

poster. The advertising message posted on an advertising structure.

poster panel. An outdoor advertising structure on which 30-sheet or eight-sheet posters are displayed; synonymous with *stand*.

poster showing. A group of posters carrying an advertiser's message.

posting date. The date on which the plant operator is scheduled to start posting a showing.

posting date leeway. The period of time within which a posting should be completed. Because of inclement weather or scheduling difficulties, it is sometimes impossible to post on the scheduled posting date. If posters are put up within five working days after the posting date, they are not considered late. Also, posters may be put up within five days prior to the posting date without violating the contract agreement. The 30-day display period starts with the actual date of posting.

potential viewer family. One or more persons from a family who pass a typical poster showing, which they may or may not have seen but have had an opportunity to see.

pounce. An actual-size pattern of an original design which is used in the paint studio to ensure that the proper dimensions are used.

preferred position. Painted displays of outstanding value located at downtown points with great circulation.

prepasting. A technique for applying paste to the back of posters using modern machinery and a conveyor belt system of production. Posters are prepared for posting, sealed in plastic bags, and stored until the posting date.

proposal. A formal recommendation to a client or an advertising agency proposing the purchase of outdoor advertising

public service copy. Display copy of a civic or philanthropic nature posted free of charge in the interest of community welfare.

purchase. *See* buy.

rain lap. A posting method in which the top sheets overlap the lower ones so that rain does not run under the paper and loosen it.

rate book. A book that lists the prices of posters and painted bulletins.

reach. The actual percentage of the market covered by a showing.

reflector shades. The incandescent light fixtures attached to an illuminated outdoor advertising structure; synonymous with *cans.*

regular. An unilluminated poster or paint unit.

renewals. Posters sent to plant operators in excess of the exact number required for posting; used to replace any posters that become damaged.

repaints. The repainting of painted displays using either new copy or the same copy.

reposting. To repost or redo a panel with the same copy.

representative showing. An intense poster display generally used to provide complete market coverage.

ride the boards. To review the physical characteristics of a sign, i.e., its attractiveness, the presence of obstacles to vision, normal visibility to drivers, and the length of time the sign can be observed easily.

rotary paint. A painted bulletin with copy that is moved to six different locations during a 12-month period.

rotating plan. The periodic movement of an advertiser's painted bulletin copy to different painted bulletin locations on major arterials in the market area. The copy is usually moved every 30 or 60 days.

royal facing. A painted bulletin embellishment which produces the same effect as magazine bleed printing, i.e., there is no molding or frame. The enlarged display area is affixed to the face of the sign and extends beyond the molding of the bulletin.

sale. Within the sign industry, the renting of a sign by an advertiser. *See* buy.

sales clause. A clause that gives the lessor the right to terminate the lease if the property is sold.

sales comparison approach. A valuation approach in which an appraiser derives a value indication by comparing the property being appraised to similar properties that have been sold recently, applying appropriate units of comparison, and making adjustments based on the elements of comparison and the sale prices of the comparables.

sales or lease rider. An addition to a lease written on a separate piece of paper and attached to the lease.

Scotchlite. Registered trade name for a material that, when exposed to the headlights of a car, reflects the light allowing the message to be read by night drivers.

secured unbuilt. Describes a location where land has been leased, but advertising structures have not yet been built.

selling companies. Companies that operate like advertising agencies but confine their activities to the outdoor medium. They usually sell directly to advertisers, place the business they secure with plant owners, and handle the complete servicing of outdoor advertising campaigns.

setback. The distance from the center of the traffic approach lane to the site of the signboard; usually less than 150 feet.

shot. A location suitable for outdoor advertising.

showing. A group of posters of a particular intensity (i.e., number of panels) carrying an advertiser's message. For example, a number 100 showing consists of a number of poster panels distributed on major traffic arterials throughout a defined marketing area; it has the ability to reach, in one day, a number of people approximately equivalent to the total market population and to develop an average frequency, during 28 days, in direct proportion to the motoring habits of the market population.

show-through. Copy from a previous poster that is visible, or shows through, after a new poster has been posted.

signage. A group of signs.

silk screen. A method of printing used in the mass production of posters. A stencil (design) is cut from a plastic sheet and affixed to silk which is stretched on a frame. To transfer the design onto paper, the frame is positioned over the paper and paint is applied to the silk and forced through the openings in the silk weave using a squeegee.

snipe. A sheet posted over a section of a poster, showing a price, a date, or other timely information; synonymous with *overlay*.

space position value (SPV). A rating of the visibility of a poster measured using the SPV rating system, which has been replaced with the OVRS. *See also* Outdoor Visibility Rating System.

special showing. A showing for which unpublished, but premium, rates are obtained for a small number of panels.

spectacular. A painted bulletin embellished with electrical effects such as flashing letters or neon lighting.

speculation lease. A lease taken in anticipation of the opening of an advertising location.

spotted map. A map provided by the plant operator showing the locations of the poster panels and/or painted bulletins in a showing.

SPV. *See* space position value.

stand. An advertising structure on which posters are displayed; measures 12 feet, 6 inches x 25 feet overall, with a display area of 10 feet x 22 feet; synonymous with *poster panel*.

standardized industry. A segment of the outdoor advertising industry that owns, maintains, and rents signs of standard design and size.

standard showing. One of the recognized poster coverage intensities: i.e., minimum, representative, or intensive.

standard structures. Various types of outdoor advertising structures which have been designed and built according to standards approved by the Outdoor Advertising Association of America, Inc.

standards of practice. Methods of operation for both poster and painted display plants approved by the Outdoor Advertising Association of America, Inc.

store bulletin. A painted display bulletin located on a side wall of a retail store in an urban shopping area; has a standard height of 9 feet, 10-1/2 inches overall and may vary in length from 11 feet, 6 inches to 25 feet, 3 inches.

streamliner. A new type of painted bulletin developed to give a modern atmosphere to an advertisement.

substitution, principle of. The appraisal principle that states that when several similar or commensurate commodities, goods, or services are available, the one with the lowest price will attract the greatest demand and widest distribution.

suburban bulletin. A painted display bulletin located in a suburban area.

target. A small sign that partially obstructs the view of a panel.

Traffic Audit Bureau (TAB). An independent, nonprofit organization supported by advertisers, agencies, and plant operators which audits the circulation values of outdoor advertising.

trim. The molding on painted bulletins and poster panels.

trivision. A painted display embellishment that employs triangular louver construction to display three different advertising messages in a predetermined sequence; synonymous with *multivision*.

unilluminated panel. A poster panel without overhead lights.

unitized construction. The prefabrication of poster panels in the yard facilities of some plant operators. Unitized construction eliminates on-site assembly of poster panels. Once the poster panel has been assembled in the yard, it is transported by truck to the location and affixed to steel posts previously set in place An initial poster is placed on the panel while it is still in the yard, thereby eliminating a special billposting trip.

vehicle load. *See* load factor.

voluntary regulations. Standards of practice that govern the placement and operation of outdoor plants in a manner consistent with the public policy of the business.

wall bulletin. A painted display bulletin attached to a wall, usually in an urban area.

whole property. *See* larger parcel.

zone. An area partitioned by ordinance and reserved for a specific land use.

BIBLIOGRAPHY

Appraisal Institute. *The Appraisal of Real Estate.* 10th ed. Chicago: Appraisal Institute, 1992.

Berry, Haskell, Jr. "Monopoly Property—Monopoly Value." *The Appraisal Journal* (October 1984).

Friedman, Edith J. *Encyclopedia of Real Estate Appraising.* 3d ed. Englewood Cliffs, N.J.: Prentice-Hall, 1978.

International Association of Assessing Officers. *Property Assessment Valuation.* Chicago: International Association of Assessing Officers, 1977.

_____. *Property Appraisal and Assessment Administration.* Chicago: International Association of Assessing Officers, 1990.

Landretti, Gregory L. "Economics, the Real Estate Process, and Appraisal Models." *Assessment Digest.* (July/August 1991).

Sackman, J. and R. Van Brunt. "Compensability of Outdoor Advertising Structures and Billboards." Section 23.03. *Nichols' The Law of Eminent Domain.* Rel. 35, 10/92 . Pub 243/460. (New York: Matthew Bender).

Sutte, Donald T., Jr. *The Appraisal of Roadside Advertising Signs.* Chicago: American Institute of Real Estate Appraisal, 1972.

Wagner, James and David Baker. "The Valuation of Outdoor Advertising Structures: A Mass Appraisal Approach." *Appraisal Digest*. (July/August 1991).

Wallace, Steve L. "Market Value and Outdoor Advertising Structures: Outdoor Advertising Revisited." *Assessment Digest*. (May/June 1993).

Western States Association of Tax Administrators. *Appraisal Handbook*. Western States Association of Tax Administrators, 1989.